UNBELIEF – The _ONLY_ Hindrance to Receiving from God

Shawn Machen

*T*his book is dedicated to my wonderful wife, Andrea. I will forever be grateful for the love and support that you have given me as we have pursued the purpose and plan of God together. It has been an awesome and glorious journey, and I truly believe that this is only the beginning. Thank you for completing me.

Acknowledgments

With special thanks:

To Derrick and Miranda Griffie for their loyal friendship and support, especially during the writing of this book.

To Denise Bailey and Kimberly Patterson for their help and advice in the editing of this project.

To Kerri Pruitt for her guidance in the publishing of this book.

CONTENTS

INTRODUCTION

G rowing up in church, I have heard all kinds of doc-
trines and beliefs concerning God and His Word.
Unfortunately, many ministers of the gospel have wasted a
lot of time talking about a judgmental God who is angry at
the world. I was listening to a TV evangelist one day after
Hurricane Katrina hit New Orleans, Louisiana in August of
2005, and I was very disappointed in what he said. He was
talking about how God sent that hurricane to New Orleans
because of the sin that was present in that city. The minister
also spoke emphatically about how God was judging New
Orleans with great destruction and pain. Statements like these
couldn't be any further from the truth. It was in that moment

the Holy Spirit said to me, "Tell the world and My people that it is easy to follow Me. Tell them that I am here to help them, never to judge them. All they have to do is believe My words and nothing will be impossible to them. Tell them it's EASY!"

I like it when things are easy, don't you? You might be thinking, "Well that sounds good, but nothing is easy, especially when you are serving God." When actually, Matthew 11:30 says, *"For my yoke is EASY, and my burden is light."* So if Jesus says it is easy, then why does it seem so hard at times? First you must understand where hardship, destruction, and pain come from. John 10:10 says, *"The thief cometh not, but for to steal, and to kill, and to destroy: I am come that they might have life, and that they might have it more abundantly."* God's desire for you and your family is to live a glorious life here on the earth with peace, prosperity, and well being. Satan tries to keep you from experiencing God's abundant life through any tactic and obstacle he can throw your way, but the devil cannot touch you if you are applying your faith with the Word and standing on God's promises. Someone might ask, "What about Job?", or "What about Paul's thorn in the flesh?" The answer is simple, and in plain sight in the Bible. God did not cause or allow bad things to happen to them. Job and Paul did not mix faith with God's promises; as a result, Satan was able to take advantage of them. We will discuss both cases in detail later in the book, but it is important to remember that God is always on your side. Satan is your enemy, not God. When you mix faith with what the Bible says and eliminate all unbelief, you will be able to win in every area of your life.

The Roller Coaster Life

A lot of Christians I know live in the "ups" and "downs" of life. This is what I call the "roller coaster life." They feel good for a while, and then they get sick; they start saving a little money, then something breaks and the repair cost depletes their savings, and so on. In fact, most people have become so accustomed to living this way, they begin to expect it. God doesn't want you to live this way. Deuteronomy 28:13 says, *"And the Lord shall make thee the head, and not the tail; and thou shalt be ABOVE ONLY, and thou shalt not be beneath..."*

It's time to get off of the roller coaster and get stable in God. Let me ask you a question: what do you believe? Think about it. What you believe affects your actions, and your actions produce results, both good and bad. Satan tries to corrupt your belief system so you will have a hard time receiving from God. There are many Christians that are going to heaven, but they live a defeated life here on the earth. Unbelief is the problem. This is why the Lord told me to write this book: to reveal the real reason why a Christian doesn't receive from God. The world is full of unbelief, but you don't have to partake of it. Once you choose to have only faith in God and what He says, then your life will be full of happiness, joy, prosperity, and health. All of the promises of God are yes, and in Him, Amen!

Chapter 1

Because of Your Unbelief

And when they were come to the multitude, there came to him a certain man, kneeling down to him, and saying,

Lord, have mercy on my son: for he is lunatic, and sore vexed: for ofttimes he falleth into the fire, and oft into the water.

And I brought him to thy disciples, and they could not cure him.

Then Jesus answered and said, O faithless and perverse generation, how long shall I be with you? How long shall I suffer you? Bring him hither to me.

And Jesus rebuked the devil; and he departed out of him: and the child was cured from that very hour.

Then came the disciples to Jesus apart, and said, Why could not we cast him out?

And Jesus said unto them, *BECAUSE OF YOUR UNBELIEF*: for verily I say unto you, If ye have faith as a grain of mustard seed, ye shall say unto this mountain, Remove hence to yonder place; and it shall remove; and nothing shall be impossible unto you.

Howbeit this kind goeth not out but by prayer and fasting.

Matthew 17:14-21

T he word "unbelief" means *faithlessness, disbelief, or want of faith.* The disciples were trying everything within their own power to set the child free, but the Bible declares that they were unable to get him delivered from the demon. When the disciples asked privately why they were unable to get the job done, Jesus said, *"Because of your unbelief!"* I know many Christians who are trying with all their might and strength to get the devil off of their backs, but they can't ever seem to get ahead in life. God gave us the provision and the power to obtain success, healing, and financial freedom through the application of faith in His Word. Unbelief is the hindrance that keeps us from receiving the promises of God.

Oh Faithless Generation

Unbelief is the opposite of faith. The response that Jesus gave to His disciples when He heard of their inability to cast out the demon was literally, *"Oh unbelieving (faith-*

less) and corrupt generation, how long am I going to put up with you?" One can clearly see that Jesus was upset with the disciples' inability to set the child free, but He didn't leave them powerless and wondering. He gave them the answer to their problem and immediately started talking about faith and how it works.

Understanding Faith

The Bible speaks often about faith, but let's read a few scriptures to better understand exactly what it is and how it works:

Now faith is the substance of things hoped for, the evidence of things not seen.

Hebrews 11:1

This is the definition of faith. Once you understand what faith is and how it works, you will be able to put it into action and receive from God. Let's look at a few things in detail: Faith is always present tense; *"Now Faith is, or Faith is*

17

Now." Faith is never in the past, and it never operates in future tense, either; *"Faith IS"*, not Faith will be. Faith is not hoping or wishing; it is expecting. When you break down the definition in its complete meaning in the Greek, Hebrews 11:1 reads, *"Now faith (conviction, persuasion, believing) is the substance (fundamental and essential part) of things hoped for (earnestly expecting), the evidence (support and assurance) of things not seen."* Faith does not rely on the natural senses. Faith simply believes the spoken Word of God. Most people refuse to believe something unless they see it with their natural eyes. They say things like, "I'll believe it when I see it." This is unbelief, the very opposite of faith. They are acting just like Thomas did when he refused to believe that Jesus had risen from the dead. Jesus said to Thomas in John 20:29, *"Because thou hast seen me, thou hast believed: blessed are they that have not seen, and yet have believed."* Faith is believing in the unseen, and that's why II Corinthians 5:7 says, *"For we walk by faith, not by sight."* It's not "Seeing is Believing", but rather, "Believing is Seeing."

That if thou shalt confess with thy mouth the Lord Jesus, and shalt *believe* in thine heart that God hath raised him from the dead, thou shalt be saved.
For with the heart man *believeth* unto righteousness; and with the mouth confession is made unto salvation.
Romans 10:9-10

But without faith it is impossible to please him: for he that cometh to God must *believe* that he is, and that he is a rewarder of them that diligently seek him.
Hebrews 11:6

And Jesus answering saith unto them, Have faith in God.
For verily I say unto you, That whosoever shall say unto this mountain, Be thou removed, and be thou cast into the sea; and shall not doubt in his heart, but shall *believe* that those things which he saith shall come to pass; he shall have whatsoever he saith.
Mark 11:22-23

In all three of these scriptures, the word "believe" is mentioned. Believing or having faith is the only way to receive from God. A person receives salvation by believing in his heart and saying with his mouth that Jesus died for his sins. The way a person receives salvation is the same way a person receives healing, peace, breakthrough, etc. He must believe it in his heart and say it with his mouth. What you believe is important in everything you do. Your belief system affects your actions, then your actions produce results, both good and bad. It is important to believe only what the Word of God says. When you speak and act on what the Bible says instead of what the world says, you will receive everything God has promised you.

God is Good All the Time

Too many Christians are confused about whom God is. They believe that He exists, but they do not believe that He rewards them all the time. A reward is something good, something that is beneficial. The only way a person can come to God is through faith. According to Hebrews 11:6, the requirement of faith is to not only believe that He exists, but to also believe that He is good all the time. Once you come to God with this knowledge, you will be able to stand against

anything that tries to steal, kill, or destroy (John 10:10).

How God anointed Jesus of Nazareth with the Holy Ghost and with power: who went about doing _good_, and healing all that were oppressed of the devil; _for God was with him._

Acts 10:38

The only way to believe in God and His goodness is to

have complete trust in Him. You wouldn't trust any person

in this world if that person lied to you, or tried to hurt you

in any way, would you? And you wouldn't put your trust in

someone if you didn't know them either. God wants us to

know Him. He wants us to trust Him in everything. The Bible

tells us that God was with Jesus when He went about doing

good. It also says Jesus healed everyone that came to Him

that was oppressed of the devil. You will *not* find one place

in the Bible where Jesus did something bad to anyone. Also,

you will *not* find that He ever allowed someone to remain

sick or in pain for a while so that He might teach them something through their trial. Anyone that came to Jesus in faith, believing and trusting that He would deliver him, received from Him every time. God is good all the time, and He is the same yesterday, today, and forever (Hebrews 13:8).

The devil is your adversary, and he is as a roaring lion seeking for someone to devour (I Peter 5:8). Anything that tries to steal, kill, or destroy comes from the devil, and God **never** uses the devil to carry out His plan in your life. The easiest way to determine what comes from God and what comes from Satan is by determining what is good and what is bad. ***Everything bad comes from Satan, and everything good comes from God.*** Sickness is bad because it tries to steal, kill, and destroy. Poverty is bad, depression is bad, pain is bad, debt is bad, etc. Health is good, happiness is good, prosperity is good, peace is good, and so on. It is important to make this easy distinction in your life; in doing so, you will learn to have confidence and faith in God. If you believe that God allows or causes bad things to happen to you in order to teach you something, you will never be able to experience the true freedom and abundant life that Jesus promised you here on the earth. It is impossible to have true faith in God unless you know with full assurance that God is for you and He is good all the time.

If You Have Faith as a Grain of Mustard Seed

Jesus said the reason the disciples were unable to cast out the demon was because of their unbelief. Then He immediately started talking to them about faith and how it works: *"If ye have faith as a grain of mustard seed, ye shall say unto this mountain, Remove hence to yonder place; and it shall remove; and nothing shall be impossible unto you."* Most people have only focused on the mustard seed that is mentioned in this scripture, and they have said things like, "Oh, if I could just get that mustard seed faith...", and they miss the purpose of what Jesus said altogether. The point that Jesus made is to know and understand faith "like a seed."

Think of it this way: <u>a seed knows only one thing</u> – to produce. Because a seed knows only one thing, it expects only one thing, and that is what it obtains. Here is a better way to understand exactly what Jesus said: *"If you had expectancy or if you believed like a seed does, you would speak to this mountain and it would remove, and nothing would be impossible to you."*

A seed doesn't know the word can't. In fact, the word "can't" shouldn't even be a part of a Christian's vocabulary. Have you ever seen a photograph of a tree growing out of a crevice in a boulder or a rock? The tree started from a little seed that fell in the crevice of that rock, and that seed did not know that it wasn't supposed to grow there. The seed knew only one thing, and because it knew only one thing, it expected only one thing. The seed produced even though the circumstances around it said it was impossible. What are you expecting? What do you believe? Is God able to heal your body? Is He able to save a loved one? Is He able to turn your finances around? Of course He is, but what causes His ability to become your reality is your expectation. This is what faith is all about.

When the Lord was talking to me and giving me the revelation about how faith works like a seed, I asked Him, "Lord, is this why Christians have faith failures?" I will never forget the response He gave me, and I remember the words He spoke shook my inner man. He said, "There are no faith failures. There are only unbelief failures. Faith Never Fails!" When He spoke this to me, it changed my thinking completely. Faith doesn't know how to fail. It knows only one thing just like a seed knows only one thing. Faith knows only to produce a harvest from the Word of God, and since it knows only one thing, it expects only one thing. If faith is the only thing in your heart, then the harvest of faith is the only thing you will expect; therefore, nothing will be impossible to you.

The Prayer and Fasting Question

Jesus said, *"Howbeit, this kind goeth not out but by prayer and fasting"* (Matthew 17:21). What was Jesus referring to when He used the word "kind"? There are 3 things to which Jesus was referring when He used the word "kind" in this scripture: 1.) this demon, or kind of demon, 2.) this unbelief, or kind of unbelief, and 3.) this faith or kind of faith. Most people interpret the word "kind" as only "this kind of demon", but remember Jesus was talking about the demon, unbelief, and faith when He was giving the answer to why they were unable to set the boy free. This is exactly why Jesus used the word "kind" in His explanation – to identify all three. The conclusion is this: prayer and fasting brings strength to your faith in God, and when your faith is strong, no unbelief will be able to stop you from casting out a demon.

Our goal should be to draw so close to God that no unbelief will be able to stop our faith from operating. This is what Jesus was referring to when He said, *"Nothing shall be impossible to him that believes."* Believing (having faith) is the key to receiving from God all the time.

Chapter 2

The "Second Word"

According to Romans 10:17 faith can come only one way: by hearing the Word of God. Since unbelief is the opposite of faith, it can come only one way: by hearing the word of the devil. This is what I call "the second word." Any word that contradicts what God's Word says is a second word. In the Garden of Eden, Satan came to the woman and questioned her about what God had spoken to her: *"Yea, hath God said, Ye shall not eat of every tree of the garden?"* (Genesis 3:1). The woman responded that if they ate of The Tree of Knowledge of Good and Evil, they would die. Satan said to her, *"Ye shall not surely die."* This is a second word, a word that contradicted what God said. The goal of a second

word is to produce unbelief.

**And the serpent said unto the woman, Ye shall not
surely die:**
**For God doth know that in the day ye eat thereof,
then your eyes shall be opened, and ye shall be as gods,
knowing good and evil.**
Genesis 3:4-5

A seed knows only one thing; therefore, it expects only

one thing. Adam knew only one thing before he sinned.

Adam knew only good. There was no sickness, no pain, no

hardship, and no lack until Adam believed the second word

from Satan over God's original word. The problem for most

Christians is that they <u>KNOW</u> entirely too much; they know

more than one thing. We have been taught by the system

of this world how to be afraid, how to get in debt, or how

to worry. We have been taught that getting sick is a part of

life, that being afraid is normal, and that having a mortgage

is common. According to God's Word concerning all of

these things, they are a "second word" to His original word of promise. Sickness is not from God, never has been, and never will be. God said in Exodus 15:26, *"I am the Lord that healeth thee."* When we believe what God says instead of what the world or Satan says, and act in faith accordingly, we will receive His benefits every time. Adam believed and acted on what the devil said (second word) instead of what God said (first word). As a result, he lost the benefits of God's promises.

And Jesus answered and said unto her, Martha, Martha, thou art careful and troubled about many things:
But _ONE THING_ is needful: and Mary hath chosen that good part, which shall not be taken away from her.
Luke 10:41-42

In the original text, Jesus did not call her name twice. He said "Martha!" sharply just one time. Today, there are many Christians just like Martha. They are troubled and worried about many things. When Jesus said one thing is needful, He was referring to the Word of God. Faith comes by hearing and hearing by the Word of God. A seed knows only one thing, and according to what Jesus said, only one thing is needful for us: The Word of God. Remember, Adam knew only one thing before he sinned, but when he believed the word from the devil over God's word, he lost the blessing.

Which Came First, Sin or Unbelief?

Satan came to the woman in the Garden of Eden and challenged what God had spoken. When the woman heard the "second word", she and her husband acted in unbelief by eating of the fruit of The Tree of Knowledge of Good and Evil. Unbelief came first, because they did not believe what God had spoken over what the devil said; therefore, *sin is the action of unbelief!* It is extremely important to know that Satan cannot touch anyone in any way unless there is a legal avenue for him to do so. I Peter 5:8 says, *"Be sober, be vigilant; because your adversary the devil, as a roaring lion, walketh about seeking whom he may devour."* Satan cannot touch you unless you allow him to. He must have your consent to bring anything bad into your life. Unbelief is the root cause and the legal avenue or consent that Satan uses to try to invade your life.

Another important fact about what happened in the Garden of Eden is that Adam had the opportunity to reject the "second word" before he sinned. Their eyes were not opened until they actually placed action with their unbelief by eating of the forbidden fruit. James 1:14 says, *"But every man is tempted, when he is <u>drawn away</u> of his own lust, and enticed. Then when lust hath conceived, it bringeth forth sin: and sin, when it is finished, bringeth forth death."* Unbelief is the source that tries to draw away a person to the enticement of sin, and when sin is finished, it brings forth death. This is why it is vitally important to *"Cast down imaginations, and every high thing that exalteth itself against the knowledge of God, and bring into captivity every thought to the obedience of Christ"* (II Corinthians 10:5). When the devil tries to challenge God's Word in your life, cast it down and reject it immediately. If you do this as Jesus did when He was tempted by the devil, you will stop unbelief in its tracks.

Deception and Unbelief

And the great dragon was cast out, that old serpent, called the Devil, and Satan, which *DECEIVETH* the whole world: he was cast out into the earth, and his angels were cast out with him.

Revelation 12:9

Be not *DECEIVED*; God is not mocked: for whatsoever a man soweth, that shall he also reap.

Galatians 6:7

Unbelief does not work by itself. It must have something precede it in order for it to produce. Satan tries to use the natural senses: what you hear, see, touch, taste, and smell to manipulate your mind into believing something other than the truth. Satan used these senses against the woman to deceive her from the original word from God. Most people base things only on what they can perceive with their natural senses, but Hebrews 11:3 says, *"Through faith we under-*

stand that the worlds were framed by the word of God, so that things which are seen were not made of things which do appear." In other words, everything you perceive with the five senses was created by something that you cannot see with your natural eyes.

In the Garden of Eden, Satan used all five natural senses to deceive the woman into operating in unbelief. First, Satan brought forth the "second word", and the woman *HEARD* it. Then in Genesis 3:6, *"And when the woman SAW that the tree was good for food, and that it was pleasant to the EYES, and a tree to be desired to make one wise, she TOOK (TOUCH) of the fruit thereof, and DID EAT (TASTE), and gave also unto her husband with her; and he DID EAT (TASTE)."* The only one of the five senses not mentioned in the Garden of Eden was smell, but I guarantee that if you were trying a new fruit or food for the first time, you would smell it before you took a bite of it. All five senses were used against the man and the woman in the garden. Now you can see how Satan used what the woman heard, saw, touched, smelled, and tasted to deceive her into believing his word over God's word. She operated in unbelief by trusting her natural senses over what God had spoken.

Just because something sounds or looks good, like the forbidden fruit did to Adam, doesn't necessarily mean that it is good. Just because something sounds or looks bad, doesn't mean it is bad either. You are submitted either to faith or unbelief. Whose report will you believe? Example: after a checkup, a doctor brings a report to a Christian concerning his health; he tells the patient the he has an incurable disease and doesn't have long to live. *In the natural*, this report sounds bad and looks bad. *In the Spirit*, God's Word says in Isaiah 53:5 and I Peter 2:24, *"By His stripes, I am healed."* A negative report is always a "second word" to God's Word. If the Christian that hears the bad report chooses to believe and accept what is spoken by the doctor, then he will unfortunately keep that incurable disease and will die prematurely before God's plan is fulfilled in his life on the earth. But if he chooses to mix faith with God's Word and he submits himself to God according to James 4:6-7, then he can resist the disease that came from the devil. The incurable disease will have no choice but to flee from him. Nothing is "incurable" to God!

Satan tries to deceive you through your senses just like he did with Adam. Your senses must be retrained to submit to faith; when this happens, you will be able to receive from God. If you are not receiving something from God that you know He has promised you in His Word, then you need to check out what kind of seeds are in your heart. Galatians 6:7 says, *"Be not deceived; God is not mocked: for whatsoever a man soweth, that shall he also reap."* If you are planting "Word" seed and "world" seed, then the "world" seed, which is full of unbelief, will hinder the production of the "Word" seed. The "world" seed is a part of the "second word" that the devil uses to try to deceive your senses. My wife and I have witnessed many tremendous miracles over the years when people have simply refused the "second word" from the devil and put God's Word as the final authority in their lives. The Word of God never fails, but it takes your faith, your expectation, and your action to manifest His power in your life.

Autistic Child Completely Healed

My wife and I have two very good friends who gave birth to their second child, Andrew in April, 2003. The parents are members of our church. They have learned through the teaching of the Word at World Victory Church how to believe God, how to trust Him, and how to receive from His promises. As Andrew grew, the parents noticed that he was not developing in his motor skills like their other son had developed. In fact, Andrew was over 3 years of age before he spoke his first word. They decided to take him to a specialist, and as a result, Andrew was diagnosed with autism.

My wife and I talked to both parents on the phone when we heard this diagnosis. We encouraged them to *not* accept this "second word" that stood against God's promise of a perfect and healthy child. They diligently planted the seeds of the Word of God, and they would not allow the doctor to label their son as autistic. After receiving the diagnosis, we came together as a church body and prayed for Andrew. We spoke directly to the dumb and deaf spirit that was attacking his body, and I remember how God instructed me to speak to his ears and to command his hearing to be made perfect. As we laid hands on him, we saw the power of God move, and we physically felt the anointing of God in Andrew's little body. In the same week, Andrew's parents began to see a change - *a God change!* Andrew started speaking in sentences for the first time, and he became more attentive to his surroundings. Andrew was acting normal! When they took their son back to the doctor, he was amazed. Today, Andrew is completely normal and the doctors have confirmed it!

Here is an important note: before Andrew's healing, there was a constant battle in the parent's minds. Thoughts from the devil were trying to tell them that what the medical professional had spoken was a fact. In the medical world, autism is irreversible. Not only did the parents hear what the doctor said, but they also saw with their own eyes the problems that their son was having. Satan was trying to deceive them into believing that their youngest child would always have autism, never living a normal life. Praise God the parents did not accept what the devil had to offer. They put the Word of God into action by first casting down the imaginations that came from the devil. Because they refused the "second word", God was able to completely heal and deliver their son from Satan's hands. The curse of autism was nullified and cancelled out of Andrew's body! Jesus reversed the curse! Galatians 3:13 says, *"Christ hath redeemed* (rescued) *us from the curse of the law, being made a curse for us; for it is written, Cursed is every one that hangeth on a tree."* If the parents would have accepted the diagnosis, their son would be autistic today. Instead, they mixed (applied) their faith in agreement with God's Word and Andrew is completely perfect and normal!

Hearing and Seeing

God delivered just Lot, vexed with the filthy conversation of the wicked:
(For that righteous man dwelling among them, in *SEEING and HEARING,* vexed his righteous soul from day to day with their unlawful deeds.)
II Peter 2:7-8

Hearing and seeing are the two most important senses out of the five. When you are able to control what you hear and what you see, the other three senses will fall in line. Even though Lot was a good person, he heard and saw bad things. He surrounded himself with evil, and what he heard and saw affected his morals and his actions. Lot became corrupt in his thinking even to the point that he offered to give his own virgin daughters to the perverted men of that city when they tried to make Lot give up the two men (angels) that came to rescue his family. What you hang around, you will become! As a believer, you cannot afford to hang around people that are always talking "doom and gloom", poverty, sickness, etc. You can't even afford to hang around someone that curses all the time. After a while, those seeds will be planted in your heart and you will start cursing just like that person. Your surroundings affect your hearing, and what you hear will either build your faith or it will build your unbelief. Hearing and seeing are the first two senses that are mentioned in the Bible that Satan used against the woman in the Garden of Eden. Jesus spoke of their importance as well:

Take heed what ye <u>hear</u>: with what measure ye mete, it shall be measured to you: and unto you that <u>hear</u> shall more be given.
Mark 4:24

The light of the body is the <u>eye</u>: if therefore thine <u>eye</u> be single, thy whole body shall be full of light.
Matthew 6:22

What you hear and what you see tries to tell your mind what is real and what is not real. Most people have accustomed themselves to living by only natural laws. If they don't see it, they refuse to believe it. But in God's Word, there are spiritual laws that control every natural law. In fact, based on what the Bible says, did you know that what you hear actually affects how you see things? They are spiritually connected. Look at this next scripture carefully:

And Ahab told Jezebel all that Elijah had done, and withal how he had slain all the prophets with the sword.
Then Jezebel sent a messenger unto Elijah, saying, So let the gods do to me, and more also, if I make not thy life as the life of one of them by tomorrow about this time.
And when he *SAW THAT*, he arose, and went for his life..."
I Kings 19:1-3

Elijah, the mighty prophet of God, had just called down fire from heaven after he made the challenge to the 450 prophets of Baal. After he made a show of God's power before all the witnesses that stood around, Elijah had all 450 false prophets executed. This same man, who demonstrated

God's awesome power, ran in stark terror when he SAW what he HEARD. He didn't see this with his physical eyes. Elijah saw this in his mind. What he heard painted a picture in his inner man, and he accepted it. Elijah was deceived by what he heard, and this adversely affected what he saw and how he acted. Unbelief comes by hearing the word of the devil, but you don't have to receive it. Elijah should have rebuked that word and cast it down; instead, he allowed it to produce fear in his life. Adam should have rebuked the word from the devil in the Garden of Eden; instead, he allowed it to dominate his senses and control his actions as well.

Here is another example of how hearing affects how a person sees things: Have you ever known people that were unfaithful to their spouse? Did you ever see the person they were committing adultery with? I don't mean this to sound ugly, but in many cases, the person with whom they were committing adultery, was not very attractive at all. Do you know why? Satan deceived them through what they heard, and this affected what they saw. Adultery doesn't just happen! These people allow themselves to get bogged down with the cares of this life, and they become dissatisfied with their partner. Satan then tries to gain an advantage by using an old fling or someone at work like a secretary or boss to whisper "sweet nothings" into their life. Before they even realize it, they are in adultery and have ruined their lives. I've seen it before and thought just like you have: "What in the world were they thinking? That person is not nearly as attractive as the person they married!" This is why Jesus said, *"Take heed to what you hear"* (Mark 4:24). What you hear will affect how you see things.

There is a life in the Spirit that is so far beyond what you can see in the natural, and God wants you to experience this life more than you have ever wanted to yourself. To walk in the fullness of God, you must take off the deceptive blinders from this world and believe <u>only</u> the Word of God. Have you noticed how television is being used by the devil to try to manipulate your senses into believing something other than the real truth? TV programs are teaching that divorce, adultery, debt, anger, and strife are a normal way of life; this is a warped way of thinking. Commercials are directed toward sickness, debt, and hardships. The news media reports bad things more than it does good things; not to mention all the fear it produces in people's hearts as they listen to it. When you plant bad seeds in your heart (spirit man), then bad harvests will produce in your life, because *"out of the heart are the issues of life"* (Proverbs 4:23). Think of your heart as your garden. What you plant in your garden is what it will produce. This is why Proverbs 4:23 also says *"to keep (guard) thy heart with all diligence..."* If you want only good things to come forth in your life, then you must plant only good seeds.

This book of the law shall not depart out of thy mouth; but thou shalt meditate therein day and night, that thou mayest observe to do according to all that is written therein: for then thou shalt make thy way prosperous, and then thou shalt have good success.

Joshua 1:8

If you plant only "Word" seed, then your heart will produce only "Word" harvest; but if you mix "Word" seed with "World" seed, then you will have a mixed harvest. This is why so many Christians live a "roller coaster" life. Jesus said it best in Mark 4:18-19, *"And these are they which are sown among thorns; such as hear the word, And the cares of this world, and the deceitfulness of riches, and the lusts of other things entering in, choke the word, and it becometh unfruitful."* This is from where the "ups" and "downs" come. What you hear affects what you see, and what you see is what you get! What are you seeing? Are you seeing things the way the news media portrays them to be? Do you see your health the way the doctor sees it? Or do you see things the way God sees them? I encourage you to shut off all voices of unbelief in your life. You can start a new life today by simply seeing yourself the way God sees you. See yourself through the image of His Word. See yourself through the eyes of Jesus.

Chapter 3

Retraining Your Senses

But strong meat belongeth to them that are of full age, even those who by reason of use have their senses _exercised_ to discern both good and evil.

Hebrews 5:14

The word "exercised" in this passage of scripture comes from the Greek word that simply means *trained*. There is a lot of corruption in this world. As a believer, you should not be affected by the corruption and the problems that surround you. God has anointed you to be different. He has called you to live above the standards of this natural world. When worldly people base their reality on what they hear and see, Christians should be walking by faith and in the Spirit. The only way to walk this way is by retraining the natural senses. The natural senses must be submitted to the Word of God.

Before sin, Adam knew only one thing - Good! When he believed the devil's word over God's word, his eyes were opened to <u>Know</u> both good and evil. Under the new covenant through Jesus, we can now retrain our senses to <u>Discern</u> both good and evil. This is possible by rightly dividing the Word of Truth while meditating in His Word every day and every night. (II Timothy 2:15, Joshua 1:8). This is so vital to your walk with God, and it will determine your success here on the earth. As crazy as it sounds, there are many people, Christians included, that have a hard time discerning between what is good and what is bad. Too many people believe that God causes or allows bad things to happen in this world for humility and teaching purposes. This is improper discernment of God and His goodness. When a person's discernment is corrupted, his walk with God will be hindered by the enemy. The Bible is clear in revealing the nature of our

Heavenly Father as good all the time. John 10:10 says, *"The thief cometh not, but for to steal, and to kill, and to destroy: I am come that they might have life, and that they might have it more abundantly."* If there is something bad happening in your life, if it is stealing from you, or if it is trying to hurt or destroy you, it is from the devil. Everything bad comes from Satan and everything good comes from God. When your senses become trained to understand and see with clarity what the Word of God says, you will learn how to have dominion over the elements of this world.

Peter Walked on Water

In Matthew 14, there is a true account of Jesus walking on water as He was coming to the disciples in the boat. Twelve men were in the boat, but only Peter decided that he could walk on the water to go to Jesus. What made Peter believe that he could walk on water? The answer: Peter saw someone else doing it. His senses became retrained into believing that walking on water was a possibility. Faith dominated his natural senses as long as his eyes were fastened on Jesus. When Peter looked at the circumstances around him, his senses overruled his faith and he began to sink. The Bible says, *"When he saw the wind boisterous, he was afraid..."* In other words, Peter was moved by what he saw. Peter stopped believing the moment he took his eyes off of Jesus. God wants us to walk above the problems of this world, but the only way to do this consistently is by keeping our eyes on the Word of God.

Wherefore seeing we also are compassed about with so great a cloud of witnesses, let us lay aside every weight, and the sin which doth so easily beset us, and let us run with patience the race that is set before us,
LOOKING unto Jesus the author and finisher of our faith...
                                                  Hebrews 12:1-2

As long as your eyes are where they should be, the rest of your body will follow. Peter took his eyes off of the Word, and this caused him to sink. Proverbs 4:25 says *"Let thine eyes look right on, and let thine eyelids look straight before thee."* Jesus is the author (captain and leader) and finisher (completer) of your faith. The only way to keep your senses submitted to your faith is by choosing to keep your eyes on Jesus and His Word. If you were to talk to Olympians that run track, they will tell you that they have been trained to keep their eyes on the finish line. If they look to the left or to the right, even for just a moment, it will slow them down and could cost them the victory that they have trained for. There are a lot of distractions in this world that Satan tries to use to slow people down. Believers should refuse to be moved by the "winds" and the "waves" of this world, and they must learn how to hold fast to the profession of their faith in order to have complete victory (Hebrews 10:23).

In Mark 5, there was a man by the name of Jairus that came to Jesus and said, *"My little daughter lieth at the point of death: I pray thee, come and lay thy hands on her, that she may be healed; and she shall live."* Jesus went with Jairus to heal his daughter, but as they were going, someone came from Jairus' house and said that his daughter had died. When Jesus heard this "second word", He immediately turned to Jairus and said, *"Be not afraid, Only believe."* Jesus said this to him to keep his senses and his confession in line. Like most people, Jairus had been trained to believe the negative, to believe the worst. If Jairus would have spoken something contrary to what he first said, then Jesus would have been *unable* to perform a mighty miracle. I realize the previous statement contradicts what most people have been taught. They think God can do anything just because He is God. Mark 6:5 says that Jesus was *unable* to do a mighty work in His own hometown because of their unbelief. It does not say that He would not do a mighty work. The Bible distinctly says that Jesus *could not* do a mighty work. He was unable to! Just as your faith will move God on your behalf, your unbelief will stop God from moving in your life as well.

I am amazed at Christians that I talk to that have a hard time receiving their healing from God simply because they base everything on what they see. When I ask them if they have ever seen Jesus or if they were present when Jesus died on the cross and rose from the grave, their answer is no, but yet they still believe. What's so hard about believing that Jesus died for their sicknesses just like He died for their sins? All they have to do is receive Him as their healer just like they received Him as their savior. It's that easy. Everything with God is easy. Our senses must be retrained to believe what faith says.

If you get a phone call at 2AM, what does your mind do? Would you think, "Oh something terrible has happened!"? Do your thoughts gravitate to the negative and always think of the worst possible thing? Or do your thoughts tend toward only good things and the positive? "Well praise the Lord, something good is coming my way, and someone couldn't wait until sunrise to tell me about it!"

Grasshopper Image

Joshua and Caleb were like that in the Old Testament. They went with ten others to spy out the promise land. Ten men came back with a negative report, but Joshua and Caleb came back with a good report. Two people were positive and the other ten were negative. Numbers 13:30 says, *"And Caleb stilled the people before Moses, and said, Let us go up at once, and possess it; for we are well able to overcome it."* Every man that went to spy out the land besides Joshua and Caleb brought up an evil report about what they saw. They even said, *"We saw the giants, the sons of Anak, which come of the giants: and we were in our own sight as grasshoppers, and so we were in their sight"* (vs. 33). They were moved by what they saw with their physical eyes, and they also had an inner image of being unable to overcome. They had a grasshopper image, and their unbelief kept them out of the promise land.

So we see that they could not enter in because of unbelief.

Let us therefore fear, lest, a promise being left us of entering into his rest, any of you should seem to come short of it.

For unto us was the gospel preached, as well as unto them; but the word preached did not profit them, not being mixed with faith in them that heard it.

Hebrews 3:19-4:2

Your inner image has everything to do with your ability to receive from God. If you believe you can, then you will; but you must retrain your senses in believing the truth, believing what the Bible says. Numbers 14:24 says, *"But my servant Caleb, because he had <u>another spirit</u> with him, and hath followed me fully, him will I bring into the land whereinto he went; and his seed shall possess it."* Caleb had the spirit of faith instead of the spirit of unbelief. Because he had faith and believed like a seed does, he received his portion of the promise land. He could have seen things the same way everyone else saw it, but his inner image was on a higher level than everyone around him. That's what faith does; it always sees things beyond the natural, and the way you see yourself is important in fulfilling God's purpose in your life. It doesn't matter one bit about your past, your education, or family history. When you became born-again, old things are passed away and all things are become new (II Cor. 5:17). Sometimes, believers have been the devil's advocate. In fact, the devil hasn't even been their greatest enemy at times; it's been their own selves. Proverbs 23:7 declares, *"As a man thinketh in his heart, so is he."* When you start believing in the Greater One that dwells in you and learn to build up that inner image of who you are in Christ, nothing will be impossible to you!

What You Don't Hate, You Will Learn to Tolerate

This is one of the greatest truths that accelerated my personal walk with the Lord, and I know it will change your life as well. If you do not hate sickness and disease, then you will learn to tolerate it and allow it to hang around from time to time. God hates sickness and disease just like He hates sin. Since we are made in His image, we should hate it also. But if you do not hate it, the natural response will be to just put up with it. Debt is the same way. There is nothing good about debt! It causes stress, worry, and fear. I saw a bumper sticker one time that read, "I owe, I owe, it's off to work I go!" I thought how true that is in most people in this world. Our thinking has been manipulated into believing that having debt is normal, that everyone has it. Our thinking must be renewed to the purposes of God. We shouldn't have a job because we must supply our living needs. Our jobs should be a source of God's blessing in our lives to support our *giving*, and our giving should be the supply of our living (Luke 6:38, Philippians 4:19). When you learn to hate what that credit card debt, car loan, and mortgage payments have done to you and your family, that's when you stop tolerating it!

In Acts 16:17-18, there was a lady that had a spirit of witchcraft that followed Paul and Silas. She was shouting with a loud voice that Paul and Silas were servants of God that were showing the way of salvation. Verse 18 declares, *"And this she did <u>MANY</u> days. But Paul, being grieved, turned and said to the spirit, I command thee in the name of Jesus Christ to come out of her. And he (the demon) came out the same hour."* Paul tolerated the demon for many days, but he didn't have to put up with it at all. When he had finally had enough of it, he dealt with it! The Bible says in Ephesians 4:27 to give the devil no place! You don't have to put up with the devices of the devil, but he will hang around as long as you allow him to.

My aunt who lives in Oneonta, Alabama told me this story one time that demonstrates exactly what I have been explaining. She woke up one morning with a horrible pain in her back, almost to the point that she could hardly stand up straight. She prayed about it but had no relief, and this went on for several days. As she was walking around the house, she finally had enough of the pain in her back. She shouted out loud, "Satan, I command you in the name of Jesus to take this pain from me, and you carry it down the street right now!" The pain left immediately. The next day, she got out of bed feeling great, and went down the street to drop off something at her neighbor's house. The neighbor came to the door and was hunched over with a grimace on her face. When my aunt asked her what was wrong, she said, "I went to bed feeling fine, but when I woke up this morning, I had a terrible pain in my back." The devil did exactly what my aunt commanded him to do; he took that back pain right down the street!

Renewing Your Mind

And be not conformed to this world: but be ye transformed by the renewing of your mind, that ye may prove what is that good, and acceptable, and perfect, will of God.

Romans 12:2

To accomplish the will of God, you must first know the will of God. Knowing God's will for your life is easy when you renew your mind to His Word, and when you renew your mind, your senses will be submitted to the authority of faith. When you accepted Jesus as your Lord and Savior, your spirit became saved, but your mind along with all five senses must be renewed to the Word of God daily; otherwise, your senses will dominate your spirit man every opportunity that you give them. This is why Paul wrote in Philippians 4:8 to *"THINK on things that are true, honest, just, pure, lovely, and of a good report."* The things about which you think or meditate affects what you believe, and what you believe affects your actions, and your actions produce results. To renew your mind, you must meditate in God's Word every day and every night. When you do this, the Bible promises that you will make your way prosperous and you will have good success (Joshua 1:8).

For the weapons of our warfare are not carnal, but mighty through God to the pulling down of strongholds;

Casting down imaginations, and every high thing that exalteth itself against the knowledge of God, and bringing into captivity every thought to the obedience of Christ.

II Corinthians 10:4-5

The way to retrain your senses is to retrain how you think. A thought by itself can do nothing, but the moment it is spoken or an action is placed with that thought, it becomes alive. This is why Jesus said in Matthew 6:31 to *"Take no thought, Saying..."* When a thought comes to your mind that contradicts the Word of God, cast it down in the name of Jesus and bring it under the submission of Christ. Have you ever noticed how Satan tries to use your thoughts against you? This is exactly how Satan tempted Jesus. He was tempted just like we are, but Jesus was without sin. Jesus spoke out loud when Satan tempted Him with evil thoughts; He said, *"It is written..."* We should combat thoughts from the devil the same way. Speak what is written: "I am healed by the stripes of Jesus, or my God supplies all of my needs according to His riches in glory by Christ Jesus!" (I Peter 2:24, Phil. 4:19). You will be unable to speak the Word of God if you do not know what the Word of God says; so start renewing your mind by hearing it, reading it, and meditating in it every moment you have. And while you're at it, if you shut off the television and other sources that are trying to produce negativity in your mind, then the harvest of the Word will produce more quickly because there is only one source of supply: the Word of God. Remember, a seed knows only one thing. If you don't like the kind of harvests you are receiving, then you are planting the wrong kind of seeds in your life. Mixed seeds produce mixed harvests as well. By planting only Word seeds, you will produce only Word harvests!

Jesus dealt with the devil two thousand years ago on the cross. He has given you the power and the authority to overcome every sickness, every hardship, and every problem that this world has to offer. Once you renew your mind and retrain your senses to know only the promises of God, your life will be full of happiness, peace, and joy. Unbelief won't have a chance to come into your life and steal from you ever again.

Chapter 4

Whosoever Gospel

And Peter calling to remembrance saith unto him, Master, behold, the fig tree which thou cursedst is withered away.

And Jesus answering saith unto them, Have faith in God.

For verily I say unto you, That *WHOSOEVER* shall say unto this mountain, Be thou removed, and be thou cast into the sea; and shall not doubt in his heart, but shall believe that those things which he saith shall come to pass; he shall have whatsoever he saith.

Mark 11:22-23

P eter and the other disciples heard Jesus speak out loud to the fig tree. When they came along the same path the next day, the fig tree was completely dried up from the roots. When Peter spoke to Jesus in amazement about what he saw, Jesus began to talk to the disciples about faith, how it works, and for whom it is available. This is a "whoso-

ever" gospel. This is not limited to just people who are called

to the five-fold ministry, and this power certainly did not

pass away when the first apostles died either. If you choose

to be a "whosoever", then you will believe what Jesus said

and begin to speak the Word of God with authority.

Your Words Are With Power

**Death and life are in the power of the tongue: and
they that love it shall eat the fruit thereof.**
Proverbs 18:21

Every word you speak is a seed. The words you speak

are either faith-filled words or unbelief-filled words. You

either speak words of life or words of death, and there is

power in every word that comes out of your mouth. This

is true whether you believe in it or not. The word "love"

in this scripture means *to have affection for and to yield.*

When you love something or yield to something, it simply

means you have an understanding of it. This is what this scripture is saying: *"Death and life are in the power of the tongue: and they that <u>understand this truth will benefit from its power</u>."* Jesus said it this way in Matthew 12:37: *"By thy words thou shalt be justified, and by thy words thou shalt be condemned."* Most Christians do not have an understanding of the value that God places on their words; if they did, they would not say over ninety percent of the things they have been saying.

When you are reading the four gospels in the New Testament, you will always find Jesus speaking the Word, speaking positive, and calling things that are not as though they were. In the case of Jairus' daughter, Jesus came to the house where everyone was crying because the little girl had passed away. When He arrived, Jesus said, *"Why make ye this ado, and weep? The damsel is not dead, but sleepeth"* (Mark 5:39). He did the same thing concerning Lazarus' sudden death. What was He doing? He was calling into existence with faith-filled words the desired end result. A born-again believer who is made in the image of God is capable of the very same thing, even to the point of moving a mountain. In order to move mountains, *"You must believe that those things which you say will come to pass, and you will have whatsoever you say"* (Mark 11:23).

Someone might say, "I believe Jesus could do supernatural things because He is the Son of God, but I can't raise the dead or move a mountain." Those words of unbelief will keep him from doing a mighty work for God. He is speaking contrary to what the Word of God speaks; therefore he will have exactly what he expects. Joshua 10:12 says that Joshua said aloud in front of all the children of Israel, *"Sun, stand thou still upon Gibeon; and thou, Moon, in the valley of Ajalon!"* As the sun was setting, Joshua spoke directly to the sun and the moon when the children of Israel were in the middle of a battle. The Bible declares that the sun and the moon obeyed his voice. The earth stopped rotating on its axis for a period of a couple of hours until the children of Israel finished the battle. This happened simply because a man spoke it into existence. That's power!

Throughout the Bible, you will find people receiving miracles from God when they believed in their heart and spoke what they desired with their mouth. There was a woman in II Kings 4 who would not speak a negative word concerning her teenage son who had suddenly died of a heat stroke. When asked about her son by the father and the servant of Elisha, she said with confidence, *"It is well!"* Because of her perseverance, she received her dead son raised back to life. The woman with the issue of blood in Mark 5 said, *"If I may touch but his (Jesus') clothes, I will be made whole."* When she placed action with what she said and touched the hem of His garment, she received her healing. When Jesus felt virtue go out of His body, He turned around and said, *"Who touched my clothes?"* What was different about her touch? It was a touch of faith that was activated by what she said. It is also interesting to note that after the woman revealed herself to Jesus, He said to her, *"Daughter, YOUR faith has made you whole."* Jesus did *not* say, My Power, My Healing, etc. He said, *"Your faith!"* Her faith was activated by the words of her mouth.

This is a "whosoever" gospel. If you choose God's promises, you will have them; but if you do not choose them, you will not have them. God has made salvation available for everyone. Jesus died on the cross for everyone, but it is not up to God who chooses His redemptive plan. People make the choice to either receive salvation or reject it. The choice belongs to them. **The choice is yours.** Healing, debt freedom, peace, love, etc. are all included in God's plan of salvation as well. To receive what has been freely given, you must believe it in your heart and speak it with your mouth. I've heard people say, "I believe that whatever God wants for me, He will make it happen; after all, He knows what's best for me because He is God." Unfortunately, a lot of people live under this kind of thinking, and that's exactly why they are having trouble in their finances, their marriage, their job, etc. Jesus said, *"By YOUR words you will be justified…"* He also said, *"Every idle word that men shall speak, they shall give account thereof in the day of judgment"* (Matthew 12:36). The word idle means *useless, barren, and inactive.* Every word that comes out of your mouth is important, and what you speak will make a difference every single day of your life. If you want good things to happen, then start speaking good things. The world and everything in it was created by words, and this very same creative power that God used in the very beginning dwells on the inside of you.

Choose To Be Chosen

Jesus said in Matthew 22:14, *"Many are called, but few are chosen"*, and in John 3:16 He said, *"For God so loved the world, that he gave his only begotten Son, that WHOSOEVER believeth in him should not perish, but have everlasting life."* God's desire is for everyone to be saved (II Peter 3:9), but it's up to you to believe in Him so you are able to receive what He has freely given. **The chosen ones are those who choose to be chosen**.

Think of it this way: Luke 10:1 declares that Jesus had seventy disciples that were working for Him in ministry. Out of the seventy disciples, there were twelve that were closer to Jesus who followed Him diligently. Out of those twelve close disciples, there were only three that Jesus took with Him into the "secret places" of God. Those three disciples were Peter, James, and John. They were chosen out of the twelve to go with Jesus to the Mount of Transfiguration; they were the only three that were taken in the house along with the parents of the little girl that suddenly died; they were the only three disciples taken to the Garden of Gethsemane before Jesus went to the cross. What made them chosen above the other disciples? They chose to be chosen! Peter wasn't perfect by any means, but when you study his life in the gospels, he was always giving 100%. Peter stepped out of the boat from the other twelve disciples when he walked on water; he mistakenly rebuked Jesus in front of everyone; he even cut off a guard's ear when they came to take Jesus away. James and John were brothers. They made the other disciples angry when they asked Jesus if God would grant them to sit on His right and left hand when He came into His kingdom; Jesus called them the Sons of Thunder, and it was John who laid his head on the breast of Jesus at the Last Supper. The point is, all seventy disciples were called, all twelve disciples were called, but only three *chose* to do things that caused them to be *chosen* by Jesus for the deeper things of God.

In the Old Testament, instruction was given for a temple to be built for the glory of God to dwell in, and it had three parts to it: Outer Court, Inner Court, and Holy of Holies. Under the new covenant, Jesus did away with the need for this temple by His shed blood. By this example, one can understand how Christians choose to live today; there are the "Outer Court" Christians, the "Inner Court" Christians, and the "Holy of Holies" Christians. You choose how far you go with God. You choose how close you get to Him. Do you want to be just a part of the seventy? Are you satisfied with being a part of the twelve? Or do you want to be so close to Jesus that He takes you into the secret places of God? It's your choice.

Chapter 5

Lack of Knowledge and Rejected Knowledge

My people are destroyed for *lack of knowledge*: because thou hast *rejected knowledge*, I will also reject thee, that thou shalt be no priest to me: seeing thou hast forgotten the law of thy God, I will also forget thy children.

Hosea 4:6

There are many different kinds of unbelief. I will discuss some of them in the next two chapters, but every kind of unbelief falls under two basic forms: **lack of knowledge** and **rejected knowledge**. Both were present in the Garden of Eden when Adam partook of The Tree of Knowledge of Good and Evil. Satan used both of them to his own advantage to take the blessing from Adam.

Lack of Knowledge

The scripture in Hosea 4:6 lets us know specifically to whom God is talking: *"MY people."* God is not talking to the world or the un-saved; He is talking to His people, or believers and followers of His Word. There are many Christians that are destroyed by the devil because he takes advantage of their lack of knowledge concerning what the Bible says. If you do not have the knowledge that God wants you to live in divine health, then how will you mix faith with His Word to receive it? If you do not have knowledge concerning God's provision in your finances, then you wouldn't know how to apply your faith with what He has said in order to receive God's *"wealth and riches in your house"* (Psalm 112:3).

I have heard people quote scriptures out of context thousands of times. When concerning the knowledge of God, many have said, *"God's thoughts are not our thoughts, and*

75

His ways are not our ways says the Lord." They quote this from Isaiah 55:8, but the problem is they have never read this scripture in its fullness for themselves. They simply quote what they have heard, but if they read verse 7, they would see and understand that this scripture was not written to the believer.

Let the <u>wicked</u> forsake his way, and the <u>unrighteous man</u> his thoughts: and let him return unto the Lord, and He will have mercy upon him; and to our God, for he will abundantly pardon.
For my thoughts are not your thoughts, neither are your ways my ways, saith the Lord.

Isaiah 55:7-8

God is not speaking to the Christian in this passage of scripture. He is talking to the unbeliever - the wicked and the unrighteous man. When a Christian quotes only part of a scripture like this one in Isaiah, it reveals that they only have part of the knowledge of God. They can then become destroyed by the destroyer (the devil) because they have a lack of knowledge. With the Bible given to us to reveal

76

God's nature and His will for our lives, there is really no excuse for a believer concerning a lack of knowledge. The truth of the matter is: we know in part only because we study in part!

Study to shew thyself approved unto God, a workman that needeth not to be ashamed, rightly *dividing* the word of truth.

II Timothy 2:15

"Dividing" means *to make a straight cut, or to dissect correctly.* You cannot know God properly if you are not properly dissecting the Bible. It is important to read every scripture in its complete context instead of taking one scripture and making a legalistic law out of it. That's what religion does, and the devil has been using this tactic even from the very beginning. He takes a part of the truth to deceive people into believing something other than the full truth of God. Jesus said, *"And ye shall know the truth, and the truth shall make you free"* (John 8:32). As I was driving to church one Sunday morning, the Holy Spirit said to me, "Tell My people to stop reading in-between the lines, and just read the lines that are set before them. There is nothing difficult about My Word."

The Bible is not difficult to understand; it's easy. It's not some book that takes a genius or a scholar to understand. The Bible is God's covenant to His people. Think of it as His love letter to His beloved. Even the book of Revelation is easy to read and understand. Most people think of the book of Revelation as a book of doom and gloom. They think it is a book that only spells out the end times and judgment on the earth. Have you ever read the book of Revelation and asked the Holy Spirit to make it easy for you? It's not a book about doom and gloom, and it's not the book of Revelations (plural), either. It's titled: The Revelation. It is a book of prophecy about Jesus and His triumph as the King of kings and Lord of lords! Revelation 1:1 says, *"The Revelation of Jesus Christ..."*, and verse 3 quotes, *"Blessed is he that readeth, and they that hear the words of this prophecy..."*

God wants you to read it so you can understand it; but you will be unable to receive the blessing that it promises if you never pick it up and read it for yourself.

The devil has deceived most people into believing that God is mysterious and it is difficult to know His ways. There is no place in the Bible that says, "God works in mysterious ways." The Bible declares the very opposite in Colossians 1:26, *"Even the mystery which hath been hid from ages and from generations, but now is made manifest to his saints."* God has made everything available for us so we can walk in His knowledge every day. He did this by sending His only begotten son to die for us on the cross. We must make the choice to seek Him, to love Him, to follow Him, and to accept what has freely been given to fully walk in His knowledge.

Paul prayed a powerful prayer for the Colossian Church:

For this cause we also, since the day we heard it, do not cease to pray for you, and to desire that ye might be filled with the knowledge of his will in all wisdom and spiritual understanding;

That ye might walk worthy of the Lord unto all pleasing, being fruitful in every good work, and increasing in the knowledge of God.

Colossians 1:9-10

If we are not supposed to know whom God is and how He does things, then why would Paul pray that the people in the church at Colosse would be filled with the knowledge of God's will and also increase in that knowledge? How can you be busy doing your Father's business if you have no idea of what your Father's business is? God wants you to know Him in a very personal way. Don't just know God for what He can do, but know Him for who He is. Refuse to just know Him as God, and learn to know Him as your father. This is why Jesus showed the disciples how to pray by beginning prayer with, *"Our Father..."* As God, He can... but as Father, He will!

The only way to know God is to draw close to God. If you seek Him, you will find Him. Unfortunately, if you are always "waiting" on God to reveal Himself in your life, you will be waiting for a while. When Moses told the people to *"Stand still and see the salvation of God"* at the Red Sea, he spoke this in error. God corrected him and said, tell the people to *"Go forward!"* (Exodus 14:15). God moves through the knowledge of His Word, and the only way you can activate this knowledge is by mixing faith and placing corresponding actions with it.

In Mark 1, there is a story about a man that was taken by his friends on a stretcher to Jesus. This man was unable to walk due to the illness that the devil had placed on him. When they arrived at the place where Jesus was preaching, they were unable to enter in the house because of the large crowd of people that were listening to His word. Many people at that point would have said, "Well it must not be the will of God for my friend to be healed." His friends did not accept this as the will of God. They climbed up on top of the house, tore a large hole in the roof, and let down their friend right in front of Jesus. They did not accept "no" as their answer. When Jesus saw their faith, He healed their friend. What was it that Jesus actually saw? He saw their actions! This is a powerful story that relates how once you receive the knowledge of God, you will be required to put that knowledge into action to gain the benefits of it.

There are many stories like this in the Bible. One of these stories is about a man named Zacchaeus in Luke 19. The Bible says he was a short man, a man of little stature. He heard about Jesus, but was unable to see Him because he was too short to see above the crowd. Did he walk away and say, "It must not be God's will for me to see Jesus"? No, but he could have said that, walked away, and missed his blessing; instead, Zacchaeus made a decision to go ahead on the path, climb up a tree, and capture that glimpse of Jesus. Zacchaeus chose to be chosen. When Jesus saw the faith of Zacchaeus in action, He called him down from the tree and resided in his house for the evening.

The renewed mind is so important to understanding the knowledge of God. When you renew your mind to the Word of God, you will know the truth and the truth will make you free in every area of your life. You might ask, "Is this really possible? Can I really know the ways of God?" The answer is yes! You should not only know His ways, but you should think just like He thinks. I Corinthians 2:16 says, *"For who hath known the mind of the Lord, that he may instruct him? But we have the mind of Christ."* All things are possible to him that believes.

God wants you to have a personal relationship with Him. He wants you to trust Him with all your heart. The only way you can trust God is if you know Him. I have two sons, and I love them with all of my heart. I want the best for them, and I want them to excel far beyond my greatest dreams. As a loving father, I have an open relationship with them. They know that they can come boldly to me and ask me for anything, anytime. They trust me because they know me. They

83

know that I would never put them in harm's way because they have assurance that I love them. Your Heavenly Father wants you to know Him. His desire is for you to have the knowledge of His will so you can come boldly to His throne of grace to receive from Him all the time. He loves you, and He always wants the best for you.

Rejected Knowledge

For Adam was first formed, then Eve.
And Adam was not deceived, but the woman being deceived was in the transgression.

I Timothy 2:13-14

In the Garden of Eden, both lack of knowledge and rejected knowledge were present. The woman was deceived by a lack of knowledge, but Adam was not deceived. This means the man knew exactly what God had spoken. He had a complete understanding of God's commandment, but decided to reject it. The man was standing *with* the woman when she took of the forbidden fruit (Genesis 3:6). Adam knew that if they partook of the fruit, it would be a direct violation to the commandment of God. Adam rejected the knowledge of God, and Hosea 4:6 says, *"Because thou hast rejected knowledge, I will also reject thee."* God is not interested in rejecting people. He loves all of us, but there is a law in motion that God will not change: the law of sowing and reaping. If you reject someone or something, it will have no choice but to reject you.

A person that hears the good news of salvation through Jesus Christ, but refuses to receive that knowledge, chooses for himself eternal damnation over eternal life. God doesn't send that person to hell. <u>God has never sent anyone to hell</u>. People choose to go to hell by rejecting the knowledge of God. The Bible says, *"Hell was made for the devil and his angels"* (Matthew 25:41). Hell was not created for people. If people choose the ways of the devil over the knowledge of God, then God has no choice but to allow them to receive hell as their eternal home. This is why God said in Deuteronomy

30:19, *"I have set before you life and death, blessing and cursing: therefore choose life, that both thou and thy seed may live."* You can choose the knowledge of God or reject it; either way, the choice is yours.

Rejected knowledge can only come forth through pride. When you know something to be true, but refuse to receive it or acknowledge it as the truth, that is a form of pride. The scribes and Pharisees in the days of Jesus are good examples of this. They had the knowledge of God concerning what the prophets had written concerning the Messiah and His coming, but they still refused to believe that Jesus was that person. They saw the mighty miracles that Jesus performed with their very own eyes, but they were so full of pride and jealousy, that they ultimately had Jesus crucified. The scribes and Pharisees were people that knew what God had spoken, but rejected it in every way. This is why Jesus said to them, *"You are of your father the devil..."* (John 8:44), and *"Full well, ye REJECT the commandment of God, that ye may keep your own tradition"* (Mark 7:9).

Another example of rejected knowledge is a person that proclaims, "I am an atheist; I don't believe in God." **There is no such thing as an atheist.** A person that proclaims this is not only rejecting knowledge, but is also rejecting common sense! The Bible says in James 2:19, *"The devils also believe (in God), and tremble."* A self-proclaiming atheist is simply denying God before witnesses. He tries to convince himself of this lie so he can live his own life the way he desires with no consequences. In his heart he knows that God exists, and in his heart he knows that there are consequences for his choices as well; he rejects the knowledge of God only because he wants to be his own god. This is exactly how Satan fell from heaven; so anyone can see the origin of that seed. The Theory of Evolution came from the same seed of pride and unbelief. There is no truth to The Theory of Evolution at all, but people accept this lie as an attempt to justify the God-less choices they make. Everyone will stand before the Judgment Seat of God one day. The people that choose to follow Jesus will have their names written in the Lamb's Book of Life, and they will live eternally with the Lord. People that openly refuse Jesus, or accept a "theory" over the knowledge of God, will be judged by their own actions of unbelief.

You may not be a self-proclaiming atheist or openly reject Jesus like the religious crowd did in His day, but what about some of the simple truths He has given to believers? He told us to forgive, if we have aught against any. If you choose to hold un-forgiveness toward someone, knowing what the Bible says about it, then you are rejecting the knowledge of God. Not only is un-forgiveness a big problem in this world, but it is also a big problem in the body of Christ. It is one of the major reasons for health problems and incurable diseases that are present today. If you refuse to forgive someone, you will open yourself up to an attack from the devil.

Someone said to me one time, "Pastor, you don't know what that person did to me. I can't forgive him!" I responded, "You obviously have no idea of what Jesus did for you!" Jesus died on the cross and forgave us of everything we have ever done wrong. There is nothing in this world that any person could do to you or say about you that would compare to what Jesus went through to give you complete freedom. Even when He was on the cross, He said, *"Father, forgive them...."* (Luke 23:34). When you know what the Bible says concerning something, but refuse to do it, that is called rejected knowledge.

Receiving from God is easy, and it all starts with developing a relationship with Him. Knowing that God loves you and wants His very best for you is the beginning of developing that relationship with Him. When you meditate in the Bible every day and every night and put into action the knowledge that you have received, you will be prosperous in everything you do. If you do not have the knowledge of how

89

to deal with a specific situation, then search in His Word, and you will always find the answer. Once you find it, be sure that you do not reject the knowledge that you have gained; this will always keep the enemy at bay.

Chapter 6

No More Fear!

Fear is one of the major kinds of unbelief that people deal with every day. The world is full of fear and anxiety, but Christians should live above anything that contradicts what the Word of God says. This chapter will enlighten your understanding to this type of unbelief. It will also reveal how Satan has used fear to deceive people, and will show how fear has hindered believers from receiving God's promises.

Thou shalt not be afraid for the terror by night; nor for the arrow that flieth by day;
Nor for the pestilence that walketh in darkness; nor for the destruction that wasteth at noon-day.

A thousand shall fall at thy side, and ten thousand at thy right hand; but it shall not come nigh thee.

Psalm 91:5-7

According to God's Word, there is absolutely nothing of which to be afraid. I realize that this is a powerful statement, but it is the truth. Did you know that spiritually speaking, every fear in this world is connected to death? Think about it: a person that is afraid of heights is fearful that he will fall and die; a person that has a fear of closed in spaces is afraid that he will suffocate to death; a person that is afraid of snakes is fearful that he will be bitten and die, and so on. Fear is a type of unbelief because if someone *believed* the word that God has spoken concerning His protection over him, there would be no reason to be afraid of anything. In fact, Jesus took care of fear and its connection to death on the cross at Calvary!

Forasmuch then as the children are partakers of flesh and blood, he also himself likewise took part of the same; that through death he might destroy him that had power of death, that is, the devil;

And deliver them _who through fear of death_ were all their lifetime subject to bondage.

Hebrews 2:14-15

There is nothing good about fear. It brings stress, restlessness, and bondage. As a believer, you have the authority through the blood of Jesus and the word of your testimony to overcome every type of fear. Did you know that worry is a type of fear? I know people that worry over the smallest things, and all it does is put them in bondage. If they do not deal with worry, it will actually shorten their lifespan here on the earth. Before Adam sinned, there was no fear. He knew only one thing - faith. But when Adam chose to listen to a word from Satan and placed his action with it, his eyes were opened. Adam acted in fear and hid himself from the presence of God. Fear is never from God. Fear is from the devil, and it comes to steal, kill, and destroy.

<u>Angels All Around</u>

There shall no evil befall thee, neither shall any plague come nigh thy dwelling.
For he shall give his angels charge over thee, to keep thee in all thy ways.
They shall bear thee up in their hands, lest thou dash thy foot against a stone.
Psalm 91:10-12

Do you believe in angels? Did you know that angels are ministering spirits sent from God to minister to those that are heirs of salvation? (Hebrews 1:14). If angels are sent to protect us and to minister to us, then why are there so many Christians struggling and dealing with sickness and other problems? The answer is unbelief, and many times that unbelief comes in the form of fear. Fear works in the negative just like faith works in the positive. To overcome fear, we must renew our minds to God's Word. When we renew our minds, we will be able to cast out every fear through the perfect love of Christ (I John 4:18). Once all the fear is gone, a believer can activate the will of God by believing it in his heart and confessing it with his mouth. Angels respond only to faith, just like God does. According to Psalm 91:11-12, angels have been given assignment to protect you in everything. So if you are speaking only the Word of God with complete conviction in your heart, the angels will see to it that you are protected from any harm that exists in this world.

I never get in my car or go anywhere without confessing (speaking) Psalm 91 over me and my family, and I always speak it out loud. I learned this at a very early age when my parents would teach me how to speak the Word of God and how to expect God's angels to protect me. I grew up in a family that loved to ride dirt bikes. Almost every Saturday during the summer, my father, older brother, and I would load up our motorcycles on the trailer and head to the woods. Now this may not mean a lot to you, but in Alabama there are big hills and mountains, and we didn't just ride the easy trails for kicks. We were climbing those mountains, always looking for a challenge. I remember hundreds of people riding their dirt bikes on a given Saturday. We saw all kinds of serious injuries, even by professional riders; but in all the years that we rode dirt bikes, we had no injuries. People were amazed at our ability to climb those hills with ease even when my brother and I were just seven and eight years of age. Were we better riders at that age than those professionals that had been riding motorcycles all their lives? No, we just confessed (spoke) the Word of God, and our big, strong angels helped us climb those hills. They went with us and protected us in every way. When I played football and basketball in high school, I saw the power of God protect me in the same manner, and I never had one broken bone. Someone might say, "Well, you were just lucky." There is no such thing as luck! But there is a thing called faith! When you mix your faith with the Word and eliminate all fear and unbelief, you will receive His promises every time.

Every Seed Produces a Harvest

Here is something else every person should understand about fear and every other kind of unbelief: every harvest produces from a seed. This is true in the natural and in the spirit. When you plant a corn seed, you receive a corn harvest. A watermelon seed produces a watermelon harvest, and so on. Now in the spirit, the same thing is true: fear cannot produce a harvest unless there is a seed for the harvest to put a demand upon. Your heart is the ground. If you have spiritually planted seeds of fear in that ground, then a harvest has a legal right to produce from what has been planted. An example of this is watching scary movies. If you plant this kind of seed in your heart, then fear will have the right to produce in your everyday life. I John 4:18 says that *fear has torment.* You might think that watching a scary movie is just entertainment, but that is exactly what Satan has deceived you into believing. Fear manifests itself in many ways, but its goal is to produce torment. Not only do scary movies pro-

duce fear, but the news, television shows, and commercials

will plant bad seeds in a person's heart as well.

Be not deceived; God is not mocked: for whatsoever a man soweth, that shall he also reap.
For he that soweth to his flesh shall of the flesh reap corruption; but he that soweth to the Spirit shall of the Spirit reap life everlasting.

Galatians 6:7-8

Here is something valuable that will change your under-

standing forever: <u>You do not have a choice on what a seed</u>

<u>produces, but you do have a choice on what kind of seed you</u>

<u>plant.</u> In other words, the harvest is already in the seed. This

is the way God made it to work even from the very begin-

ning. So if you choose to plant a seed of fear in your heart,

then without a doubt, it will produce some form of torment

in your life. If you are fed up with fear having a hold on your

life, you must get rid of its source or the avenue that Satan

is using to plant that seed in your heart. If you like watching

the local news and that is the source of fear being planted in your heart, then turn off the TV. If the television is a real big temptation for you, then get rid of it all together!

My wife and I went on our first cruise in the spring of 2010, and it was definitely one of the best vacations we ever had. One week before the cruise, we were watching television together in the evening and we happened to have the channel on one of the news stations. The news media began reporting how there were several cruise ships that had recently been battered by "rogue" waves. They even had amateur videos of the occurrences from vacationers on the cruises. I remember my wife standing up and saying out loud, "I rebuke that in the name of Jesus, and it will not come near us!" This is what the Bible means when it says to *"Cast down imaginations, and bring into captivity every thought to the obedience of Christ."* The seed of fear that the news media planted was trying to produce a harvest of torment. To be completely honest, I had to fight that fear for the whole week leading up to the cruise. Would I have had that concern or fear if I hadn't heard it reported by the news media? Absolutely not! So if I didn't have the source of the fear turned on, then I wouldn't have ever had the battle in the first place. You will always have the choice of the kind of seeds you plant in your heart. If you plant bad seeds, they will produce bad harvests. If you plant good seeds, they will produce good harvests. Many Christians have "ups and downs" simply because they have mixed seeds in their hearts, and mixed seeds always produce mixed harvests.

It's Time to Live Free from Fear

If you look at the scriptures in the New Testament, you will find the angels and Jesus always telling people, *"Don't be afraid"* or *"Fear not."* What they were doing was retraining their senses into understanding that fear is never from God. There is nothing normal about having fear in your life.

For God hath not given us the spirit of fear; but of power, and love, and of a sound mind.

II Timothy 1:7

When thou liest down, thou shalt not be afraid: yea, thou shalt lie down, and thy sleep shall be sweet.

Be not afraid of sudden fear [TERRORISM], neither of the desolation of the wicked, when it cometh.

For the Lord shall be thy confidence, and shall keep thy foot from being taken.

Proverbs 3:24-26, brackets mine

If your trust is in the Lord, there is nothing to be afraid of, not even terrorism. Since we are living in what the Bible calls the "last days", there will be many wild and crazy tactics that Satan will try to use to bring fear into the body of Christ. When everyone else is afraid, we should live in perfect peace knowing that everything is going to be just fine. If you have any fears in your life, I encourage you to strengthen yourself in the covenant of God. Stand against those fears with the authority of the blood of Jesus. It's time to be free from all unbelief, including fear!

Chapter 7

Other Kinds of Unbelief

T here are many different kinds of unbelief and all of them fall under two categories: lack of knowledge or rejected knowledge. This chapter will deal with some of the major kinds of unbelief that Christians have dealt with, and it will motivate you to pursue God in a greater way.

Doubt

And Jesus answering saith unto them, Have faith in God.

For verily I say unto you, That whosoever shall say unto this mountain, Be thou removed, and be thou cast into the sea; and shall not <u>doubt</u> in his heart, but shall believe that those things which he saith shall come to pass; he shall have whatsoever he saith.

Mark 11:22-23

"Doubt" means *hesitation, wavering, or staggering.* There is never a reason for a Christian to hesitate, waver, or stagger at anything that God says. Trusting God is the key to having faith that He will perform what He has promised, and true trust can only come through developing a relationship with Him. God will only draw close to you if you draw close to Him. If you seek the presence of God daily, there will be no place given for doubt to affect your faith and your trust in the Lord.

Have you ever heard someone say, "I doubt that!"? What they are really saying is, "I don't believe that!" Believing is the essential part to receiving from God, and it always comes from within the heart or the spirit man. Romans 10:10 says, *"With the heart man believeth unto righteousness..."* Faith is not something you try. Faith is something you do. Faith is something you live! Many times, people have missed God's blessing and answers in their lives because they are trying to accomplish things with their minds. Your mind must be renewed to the Word. Your mind must also be submitted to your heart for faith to actually produce. When Peter was walking on water, he was doing just fine as long as his eyes were focused on Jesus. The moment he looked at the elements of this world, doubt entered his heart and he began to sink. After Jesus saved him and took him to the boat, He asked, *"O thou of little faith, wherefore didst thou <u>doubt</u>?"*

It is so important to protect your heart because *"Out of it flows the issues of life."* Satan uses the cares of this world, the deceitfulness of riches, and the lusts of other things to try to choke the Word that is in your heart (Mark 4:19). To receive from God 100% of the time, you need to starve your doubts, feed your faith, and do what Proverbs 3:5 says to do: *"Trust in the Lord with all thine heart; and lean not unto thine own understanding."*

<u>The Condemned Heart</u>

Beloved, if our <u>heart</u> <u>condemn</u> us not, then have we confidence toward God.

And whatsoever we ask, we receive of him, because we keep his commandments, and do those things that are pleasing in his sight.

I John 3:21-22

The definition of "condemn" is *to find fault, blame, to judge against, or bring a sentence.* The condemned heart is one of the greatest challenges for believers today. If you do not hold judgment against yourself, then you will have confidence toward God. It's not about what you have done; it's about what Jesus has done!

I believe with all my heart that the following statement is true: believers have limited God much more in their lives than the devil could even try to do! When a Christian condemns himself in his own heart, he is saying that God's love and grace is not enough. This is unbelief. Sometimes this condemnation comes in the form of un-forgiveness. Not only should you forgive others and walk in love with them, but you must also forgive yourself. Jesus said, *"Forgive, if ye have aught against any"* (Mark 11:25). The word *"any"* includes you! God doesn't hold judgment against you. He paid the price for your past and all the problems you will ever face through His son Jesus. When you learn to walk in God's forgiveness, your heart will be clean. You will have complete assurance and faith in your heart, having the confidence to go boldly to His throne to receive from Him.

God's people have put such a legalistic hold on His grace at times, that their faith has become non-existent. With all the condemnation in the world, it's time to learn that our Savior paid the price for our mistakes and He forgives us. All we have to do is believe and walk in that forgiveness every day. Do you remember the story in the book of John where some men of the city brought a woman who was caught in adultery before Jesus to test Him concerning what the law said? Jesus spoke some powerful words to the woman after He had put all those men to shame. He said, *"Neither do I condemn (pass judgment, sentence) thee: go, and sin no more"* (John 8:11). Since we know that Jesus is the same yesterday, today, and forever, we can have the confidence that He doesn't judge us either. Jesus came into this world to judge the devil and his works, not people (John 12:31, 47).

Have you ever wondered why Satan has fought you so hard over the years? Satan is fighting against your destiny! The devil knows if he can stop or challenge your destiny, then he can possibly affect the destiny of someone else. Everything you do and every word you speak makes a difference. Satan understands how important you are to God, and the only way he can stop you is by challenging your heart. This is where your belief system resides. Learn to believe in what God's Word says concerning who He created you to be. Sometimes the devil hasn't even been your biggest enemy; it's been yourself. From time to time, Satan will send his little demons around to check on you just to make sure you are doing a good enough job of beating yourself up and bringing judgment against yourself in your heart. It's time to put the devil in his place once and for all, and have a pure heart before God. This is the only way a Christian can have

the confidence and assurance to receive from Him every

time. *"Greater is He that is in you than he that is in the*

world" (I John 4:4).

Self-Reasoning

When Jesus saw their faith, he said unto the sick of the palsy, Son, thy sins be forgiven thee.

But there were certain of the scribes sitting there, and reasoning in their hearts,

Why doth this man thus speak blasphemies? Who can forgive sins but God only?

And immediately when Jesus perceived in his spirit that they so reasoned within themselves, he said unto them, Why reason ye these things in your hearts?

Mark 2:5-8

Many Christians limit God in their lives because they

reason within themselves how things should or shouldn't

be. Faith never reasons with God. It simply believes what is

written and acts upon it. The word "reason" means *to reckon*

thoroughly, to deliberate, cast in mind, or dispute. There is

nothing wrong with asking questions, but there is always

something wrong when we cast judgment on something because of our reasoning. According to James 1:5, *"If any of you lack wisdom, let him ask of God, that giveth to all men liberally, and upbraideth not; and it shall be given him."* God wants you to ask so you can receive. The only way you can receive from God is by coming to Him with a pure heart of faith without pre-conceived ideas or religious thinking.

A religious spirit is one of the most dangerous spirits here on the earth and it comes from self-reasoning. It was the religious spirit that Jesus had the most trouble with, and ultimately, it was the religious spirit that crucified Him. When mentioning a religious spirit, you need to understand what it is. It is *not* a demon spirit or a sickness. If it was, Jesus would have cast it out or healed it. *A religious spirit is a human spirit*. When we reason within ourselves the way we think things should be, we are operating out of a religious, carnal spirit. There are a lot of Christians who have a religious spirit. They are the ones, that no matter what you show them in the Word of God, they are only going to believe what they want to believe while refusing to change.

In the Bible, there are three things that Jesus did with a person who had a religious spirit: He told them who their daddy was (John 8:44), He called them names (Matthew 23:33), and He didn't answer their questions (Mark 11:33). This is why Paul said to Timothy to *"Avoid foolish and unlearned questions, knowing that they do gender strifes"* (II Timothy 2:23). People that have a religious spirit are argumentative about what the Bible says. The Bible is easy to understand, and Satan knows the only way he can prolong his stay here on the earth is by keeping the body of Christ in disagreement.

Every denomination in this world came into existence from self-reasoning. Now I am not saying that denominations are of the devil. There is no doubt that God has used denominational churches to pour out His love and glory throughout the earth. But according to God's plan, there is only one Lord with one faith, and I can assure you that there are no denominations in heaven. Denominations are man-made, not God-made! If you take the time and research thoroughly the history and background of every denomination, you will find self-reasoning at the beginning of them all. Many denominations were started because of an individual or individuals that did not like the way things were in "their" church or denomination, and they decided to start something new.

Now I beseech you, brethren, by the name of our Lord Jesus Christ, that ye all speak the same thing, and that there be no divisions among you; but that ye be perfectly joined together in the same mind and in the same judgment.
Now this I say, that every one of you saith, I am of Paul; and I of Apollos; and I of Cephas; and I of Christ.
Is Christ divided?

I Corinthians 1:10, 12-13

Self-reasoning causes the church to be divided. When a person says, "I'm Baptist", "I'm Methodist", "I'm Catholic", "I'm Pentecostal", and so on, isn't he speaking division? It is obvious that people attend churches that are associated with different denominations, and there is nothing wrong with that; but we should be in perfect agreement with each other. If we profess Jesus as our Lord and Savior, we should be speaking the same thing with the same judgment, no matter the "kind" of church we go to. We should be Christians! We should be in perfect agreement with His Word. Satan understands the importance of agreement and harmony in the body of Christ. This is why he fights constantly to keep division stirred up among believers. Satan knows if he can divide the body of Christ, he can conquer! The most common question that I am asked concerning my church is, "What kind of church is this?" My answer is always the same: "It's a Christian church." Their next question usually is, "What denomination is your church?" I always reply, "Our church is not associated with any denomination. I searched diligently and couldn't find any denomination's mentioned in the Bible."

The Hardened Heart

Afterward he appeared unto the eleven as they sat at meat, and upbraided them with their unbelief and <u>hardness of heart</u>, because they believed not them which had seen him after he was risen.

Mark 16:14

The hardened heart produces from self-reasoning and is actually the most dangerous of all the different kinds of unbelief. The definition of the "hardened heart" is *destitution of spiritual perception, callous, blind.* When a person refuses his spiritual perception, he is in danger of not only missing the things that God has prepared for him here on the earth, but he is also in danger of missing eternal life that God has prepared for him in heaven.

Pharaoh is a good example of this in the book of Exodus. Pharaoh saw with his own eyes the power of God through the twelve plagues, but his heart was hardened. This caused him to reject God's demands that were spoken through Moses. Not only did Pharaoh lose his firstborn son, but he also lost his own life because he refused to allow his heart to be pliable.

The Pharisees and Sadducees mentioned in the New Testament also had hardened hearts. Even though they knew what the scriptures said concerning the Messiah, they rejected Him openly and refused to change.

> **Take heed, brethren, lest there be in any of you an evil <u>heart of unbelief</u>, in departing from the living God.**
> **While it is said, Today if ye will hear his voice, <u>harden</u> not your hearts, as in the provocation.**
> **For some, when they had heard, did provoke: howbeit not all that came out of Egypt by Moses.**
> **So we see that they could not enter in because of <u>unbelief.</u>**
>
> *Hebrews 3:12, 15-16, 19*

The hardened heart is an unbelieving heart, and unbelief will always keep someone from entering into God's promises. I have already discussed the importance of operating in forgiveness toward everyone, but I believe it is important to mention it again in a different context. If you carry an offense toward someone and refuse to deal with it, you are acting in unbelief in regards to God's forgiving power. This can lead to a hardened heart that could bring sickness, pain, and harm just like it did with Pharaoh.

All of the different types of unbelief that are mentioned in the Bible are easy to deal with. First, you must be born-again, and then you must renew your mind to the Word of God. Once you have renewed your mind to "think like God thinks", you will be able to place His promises into action and you will have the authority to stand against every device from the wicked one.

Chapter 8

What about Job's Affliction?

I had someone come up to me several years back and say, "Pastor, pray for me. I'm going through a 'Job' experience." I immediately said, "Praise God brother, that's exciting news!" With a puzzled look on his face, he responded, "Exciting??? What do you mean by that? I said I was going through a 'Job' experience!" I responded, "It's exciting because when you learn to pray for your friends and put yourself back under God's covering, God will turn your captivity and give you twice as much as you had before, just like He did with Job!"

Studying the Book of Job

Have you ever read the book of Job for yourself? Most Christians only quote what they have heard about Job, but have never really studied for themselves what happened to Job and why. Most people only know of all the terrible things that happened to Job. I rarely hear of people talking about how God turned Job's life right side up when Job submitted himself to God. I have heard many pastors and teachers say things like, "God allowed all those things to happen to Job." The truth is, Job stepped out of God's hedge of protection when he operated in fear. Fear is a form of unbelief, and Job's <u>unbelief</u> opened the door to the devil.

There are three things to keep in mind concerning Job when discussing him and the problems he had: *Number One*, you should never compare yourself to Job and what happened to him. Since you are not Job, you shouldn't compare your circumstances to his. If you feel you should compare yourself to someone, then compare yourself to Jesus, THE ONE who took your place on the cross and died for you. *Number Two*, Job was under an old covenant. Things were much different under the old covenant before Jesus sealed the new covenant with His own blood. A born-again Christian abides under a new and better covenant with God, and this covenant is established on greater promises. We will discuss many things about this in the latter part of this chapter. *Number Three*, remember when studying anything in the Word of God, you must *rightly divide it* (dissect it properly) and always establish it by the mouth of two or three witnesses (II Timothy 2:15, II Corinthians 13:1).

Why Bad Things Happened to Job

And it was so, when the days of their feasting were gone about, that Job sent and sanctified them, and rose up early in the morning, and offered burnt offerings according to the number of them all: <u>for Job said,</u> It may be that my sons have sinned, and cursed God in their hearts. <u>Thus did Job continually.</u>

Job 1:5

This scripture reveals to us why Satan was able to take advantage of Job and bring affliction and harm in his life. Job acted in fear concerning his children. He not only acted on that fear continually, but he also spoke it out of his mouth. Fear was in his heart, and out of the abundance of his heart, his mouth spoke (Matthew 12:34). In chapter six, I discussed the importance of eliminating every fear in your life. Fear will open the door to the enemy. Fear is a form of unbelief and it will keep anyone from receiving from God. You have been given authority over all fear, but ultimately, you have the choice whether you walk in fear or walk by faith.

For the thing which <u>I greatly feared</u> is come upon me, and that which <u>I was afraid of</u> is come unto me.
Job 3:25

The fear that resided in Job's heart is the very thing that allowed the devil to come into his life. God never removed His protection from him. Job stepped out from under God's covering. Psalm 91:1 says, *"He that dwelleth in the secret*

119

place of the most High shall <u>abide</u> under the shadow of the Almighty." Affliction, trials, and pain only exist outside of the covering of God. We must abide or stay under God's covering by choosing to remain there. This is what Jesus was referring to when He said in John 15:5, *"He that <u>abideth</u> in me, and I in him, the same bringeth forth much fruit."* A Christian chooses to stay close to God by reading and meditating in His Word and placing it into action. When he does this, the devil will be unable to touch him because he is protected by the covering of God.

Then Satan answered the Lord, and said, Doth Job fear God for naught?
Hast not thou made an hedge about him, and about his house, and about all that he hath on every side? Thou hast blessed the work of his hands, and his substance is increased in the land.

Job 1:9-10

Satan mentioned to God that there was a hedge around Job and all of his belongings. The devil is really stupid. Anyone that thinks they can overrule God and take over His position has got some serious mental problems! Satan didn't even realize that Job had stepped outside of God's protection. The hedge of protection is available for every Christian today, but it's their personal responsibility to remain within the hedge of the Lord. Ephesians 6 also gives us insight into God's protection. Verse 11 says, *"Put on the whole armor of God that ye may be able to stand against the wiles (devices) of the devil."* The subject of this scripture is the "understood you". You must put on God's armor to stand against the devil, just like you must resist the devil according to James 4:7. When you resist the devil with the understanding and authority of the name of Jesus, Satan will flee from you every time. Ephesians 6:16 says, *"Above all, taking the shield of faith, wherewith ye shall be able to quench all the fiery darts of the wicked."* As a believer, you must take what has been freely given by God and properly activate it in your life. The problem with Job's hedge was fear. When Job acted in fear concerning his family, he stepped outside of God's protective covering. His unbelief opened the door to Satan and this is why Satan was able to cause bad things to happen to him and his family.

I have people ask me all the time, "Why do bad things happen to good people?" I usually respond with a question as well: "Why do good things happen to bad people?" The answer is simple: there is a good God, and there is a bad devil. Good things come only from God and bad things come only from the devil. But in-between a good God and a bad devil are either good people or bad people, and both kinds of people makes either good choices or bad choices. As a result, their choices either bring good results or bad results in their lives. Even a bad person can make a good choice and reap the benefits from that choice. Job made a bad choice even though he was a good person. He operated in fear, and this opened the legal avenue for Satan to steal, kill, and destroy. God was not responsible in any way for his pain and suffering. God was Job's answer, not his problem.

And the Lord turned the captivity of Job, when he prayed for his friends: also the Lord gave Job twice as much as he had before.

Job 42:10

Job had some serious misfortunes come into his life when he stepped outside of God's covering. If you have ever felt alone and thought you had it bad in life, just imagine what Job was going through. He lost his children, had a serious battle with boils on his skin, and even had his own wife tell him to *"Curse God and die"* (Job 2:9). This all happened to Job in a couple of weeks time. But thank God, Job didn't stay in his misfortunes. When Job got his mind off of himself and started praying for his three friends, God was able to stop all of the attacks from the devil. When Job started praying, he submitted his actions back to faith instead of fear. His actions of faith put his life back under the covering and pro-vision of God. Job was also blessed with twice as much as he had previously. Talk about the power and goodness of the Lord! God is always your answer, never your problem.

Taking Proper Responsibility

A lot of people play the "blame" game in life. When things aren't going the way they want them to go, they should look in the mirror to find out where the real problem lies. People try to blame their spouse, their boss, their upbringing, the devil, and even God. Adam and Eve tried the same thing. When God asked Adam if he had eaten of the forbidden fruit, he answered, *"The <u>woman</u> whom <u>thou</u> <u>gavest</u> to be with me, she gave me of the tree, and I did eat"* (Genesis 3:12). Adam not only blamed his wife, but he also blamed God for giving his wife to him. When God asked the woman about the choice they made, she blamed the devil. The devil was the only one that accepted responsibility.

Adam and Eve made a choice, and that choice caused bad things to happen. They stepped outside of the covering of God by eating of the forbidden fruit. Nobody made them sin; they chose it, and because they made the wrong choice, they were separated from God. Job did the same thing when he made a choice to be afraid. He stepped outside of God's hedge of protection, and this made him vulnerable to Satan's attack.

There are three kinds of choices in this life: bad choices, good choices, and "God" choices. Bad choices will always bring bad things into your life, and good choices will bring good things into your life, but it's the "God" choices that you should seek. The "God" choices are the choices that lead you down the paths of righteousness and beside the still waters. The "God" choices are the choices that give you perfect peace in everything you do. I am not satisfied with just good things coming into my life. I want God's perfect will and His very best to overwhelm me in everything I do, and this only comes to me when I choose to listen to only His voice and stay under His protective covering.

Satan's Power Then & Now

Now there was a day when the sons of God came to present themselves before the Lord, and Satan came also among them.
And the Lord said unto Satan, Whence comest thou? Then Satan answered the Lord, and said, From going to and fro in the earth, and from walking up and down in it.
Job 1:6-7

"Sons of God" in this scripture is referring to the angels of God. The angels were coming and reporting to God on a regular basis, and Satan also showed up on this particular day. As a matter of fact, this was something that Satan did quite often before Jesus died on the cross. Satan's reason for showing up in heaven was to bring accusation against people who loved God (Revelation 12:10).

God never questioned Satan's authority or his reason for being there in heaven. He simply asked, *"From where did you come?"* Satan's answer agrees with I Peter 5:8 which says, *"Be sober, be vigilant; because your adversary the devil, as a roaring lion, walketh about, seeking whom he may devour."* The devil is your adversary, and he is always looking for a "legal" way so he can steal, kill, or destroy. The reason I use the word "legal" is because everything in this world and even in heaven works by laws. Just because Satan wants to destroy or harm you, doesn't mean that he can just jump into your life and do it. The devil cannot touch you with <u>anything</u> unless *you* give him the avenue to do so; and God is definitely not interested in "allowing" the devil to beat up on His own children either. Would you stand by and allow someone to harm one of your children or a loved one? Of course not! Yet, this is the way most Christians view their God, who they often call their father. Jesus made it plain and simple when He said, *"If ye then, being evil, know how to give good gifts unto your children, how much more shall your Father which is in heaven give good things to them that ask him?"* (Matthew 7:11).

Unfortunately, there are many people that view God as someone who sits in heaven with a judgmental attitude. They believe that God punishes all people, Christian and non-Christian alike. Many Christians even believe that God takes things from them or He allows something bad to happen to them in order to teach them a lesson when they step out of line. This is one of the biggest devices that Satan has used to deceive the heathen as well as the body of Christ. If a person believes the lies that come from the devil, he becomes powerless in this world because he has no real relationship with God. In the natural world, if you saw a father mistreating or beating on his child, you would have him arrested as an unjust and abusive parent. God is not interested in punishing or judging us. He loves us and He always wants to help us.

The truth is simple and will make you free when you receive it; God gave every person a free will. This gives you the ability and the right to choose. God "allows" you to choose between death and life, blessing and cursing (Deut 30:19). This is one of the laws that God set in motion when He created man. Adam had a choice, but he made the wrong one. Job also had a choice. Job received destruction from the devil when he made a bad choice. When Job turned from his bad choice and made a good choice, God was able to bless the work of his hand.

Job said, The Lord gave and the Lord hath taken away; blessed be the name of the Lord.

Job 1:21

God is good all the time! He doesn't take things from us, and He doesn't "allow" the devil to take things from us either. Job said this out of his lack of knowledge of God's character and the devil's character. God isn't interested in harming you in any way. He is your helper, your provider, your healer!

I have heard ministers use this scripture at funerals, and to be honest, it makes my inner man cringe every time I hear it. They quote it as if it was inspired by God. Just because someone says something about God, doesn't give us the right to quote it as if God said it. Job missed God when he operated in fear, and he also missed God when he spoke this out of a lack of knowledge. God is not the "taker" of life; He is the "giver" of life. John 3:16 says, *"For God so loved the world, that he **gave** his only begotten son..."*

I have heard other people say things like, "Well, God took that little child to heaven..." Scripture reveals to us that there are only three people that God actually "took" to heaven. They are Enoch, Elijah, and Jesus (Gen. 5:24, II Kings 2:1-11, Acts 1:9). The only people that God ever "took" out of this earth, He took their spirit man *and* their bodies. Now there is a difference between receiving someone and taking someone. God receives a person's spirit (spirit man) when he dies here on the earth if he has made Jesus the Lord of his life. God also receives the spirits of all children that die pre-maturely that have not yet reached the age of account-ability, but He has never "taken" any of them. God is the author of life, not death. If the Lord tarries (prolongs) in His return to rapture the body of Christ to heaven, and you have completed your work here on the earth, then you can commit your spirit into God's hands and God will "receive" your spirit. Stephen did this right before they stoned him in Acts 7:59. Jesus also committed His spirit to God when He died on the cross. God is always the giver, never the taker.

For the accuser of our brethren is cast down, which accused them before our God day and night.
Revelation 12:10

During the period between the fall of Adam and the resurrection of Jesus, Satan *had* a "legal" right to be in heaven at his own will, but thank God that all changed when Jesus died on the cross. The reason Satan had a legal right to be in heaven was because of Adam's sin. God had given Adam complete control of the earth (Genesis 1:28), but when Adam obeyed the devil's word over God's word, it caused the dominion that God had given to Adam to be given to Satan. At the moment of Adam's sin, Satan became *"the god of this world"* (II Cor. 4:4). By the time Job was born, Satan had been coming into heaven on a regular basis, bringing false accusations against people before God, and the only thing God could do about it was listen to it. God couldn't do anything about it because of the laws that He had placed in motion through the "first" Adam. Satan had power on earth for around four thousand years until Jesus went to the cross. In I Corinthians 15:45, Jesus is identified as the "last" Adam. When Jesus died and rose again, He stripped the devil of all the power, authority, and legal rights that Adam had placed in his (the devil's) hands.

And the Lord said unto Satan, Behold, <u>all that he (Job) hath is in thy power</u>.

Job 1:12

At the beginning of Jesus' ministry here on the earth, Satan came to Him and tempted Him with three different temptations. In the second temptation, Satan showed Jesus all the kingdoms of the world in a moment of time. Luke 4:6 declares, *"And the devil said unto him, All this power will I* give thee, and the glory of them: *for that is delivered unto*

me; and to whomsoever I will I give it." The power that God

had given to Adam was delivered into Satan's hands when

Adam sinned in the Garden of Eden. Notice God did *not* say

to Satan, "Behold, I give Job over to you." Satan already

had authority as the "ruler" of this world, and the things that

were already in Satan's power were the things that Job oper-

ated in fear over. This gave Satan the ability to bring destruc-

tion into Job's life, but thank God, we don't live under that

kind of covenant any longer!

**For this purpose the Son of God was manifested, that
he might destroy the works of the devil.**
I John 3:8

Jesus came as the "last" Adam to undo what was done

by the "first" Adam, and He took back by legal authority

what the devil had received from Adam in the Garden of

Eden. Jesus said in John 12:31, *"Now is the judgment of this*

world: now shall the prince of this world be cast out." Satan was stripped of all his power and authority when Jesus died on the cross. Jesus literally took all the power and authority from Satan, and made a show of him openly (Colossians 2:15). In other words, Jesus embarrassed the devil by making an open exhibit of him. Satan is no longer the god of this world, and the only power that he has in this world is the power that people give him! This is why Paul said in Ephesians 4:27, *"Neither give place (occupancy, space, or room) to the devil."*

The War in Heaven

And there was war in heaven: Michael and his angels fought against the dragon; and the dragon fought and his angels,
And prevailed not; neither was their place <u>found any more</u> in heaven.
And the great dragon was cast out, that old serpent, called the Devil, and Satan, which deceiveth the whole world: he was cast out into the earth, and his angels were cast out with him.
Revelation 12:7-9

In Sunday school, I was taught that before Adam was created, Satan was kicked out of heaven because he wanted to be like the Most High God. Apparently, there was a great war in heaven over this with Satan losing the battle. Sound familiar? Most Christians believe exactly the same thing, but the scriptures give us a completely different story, and with it, a much better understanding. According to Ezekiel 28 and Isaiah 14, Satan was lifted up with pride and wanted to lift his throne above God, but the war that is mentioned here in Revelation 12:7 actually took place shortly after Jesus died on the cross and was caught up (raptured) into heaven. Let's take a closer look at the scripture in its <u>chronological order</u> in Revelation 12:

And there appeared another wonder in heaven; and behold a great red dragon...
And his tail drew a third part of the stars of heaven, and did cast them to the earth.
Revelation 12:3-4

The stars in verse 4 represent the angels. John saw the devil taking 1/3 of the angels out of heaven and he cast them to the earth. There is no mention of God casting the devil out of heaven at this point in the scriptures. Satan's tail represents what was in his power or control. He took 1/3 of the angels with him because he had authority or command over 1/3. This authority was given to Satan from God before he was lifted up with pride. If you look in the Bible, you will find only three angels that have their names revealed: Michael, Gabriel, and Satan (also known as Abaddon or Apollyon). Revelation 12:7 says, *"Michael and <u>his</u> angels fought against the dragon and <u>his</u> angels."* The "his" shows authority and ownership or what they had charge and command of. This explains why 1/3 of the angels went with Satan in the beginning; Satan had authority over them. Michael has authority and command over another 1/3, and Gabriel has authority and command over the remaining 1/3 of the angels.

This further explains what happened between Genesis 1:1 and Genesis 1:2. God created everything good and perfect. Verse 1 says, *"In the beginning, God created the heaven and the earth."* After God had created the heaven and the earth, Satan decided he wanted to be like the Most High God (Isaiah 14:12-14), and he took the angels he was in command of and *cast* (sent) them to the earth. Verse 2 says, *"And the earth was without form, and void; and darkness was upon the face of the deep."* This happened a long time before man was ever created. The earth is millions of years old (even science proves this), but man has only been on the earth around six thousand years. Darkness is from the devil, and there is absolutely no darkness in God (I John 1:5). When Satan sent his angels to the earth, they completely destroyed the earth with darkness becoming the dominant force. In the rest of the first chapter of Genesis, one can read how God recreated the earth and put it under the care and authority of man, His most prized creation.

When Adam gave his authority over to Satan, God immediately put into action a prophecy of redemption. He said to Satan in Genesis 3:15, *"The seed of woman will bruise thy head, and thou shalt bruise his heel."* This prophecy was concerning Jesus, our Lord and Savior. Satan is not nearly as smart as people give him credit. All he knew was that there was a seed that would come from the woman from which he would need to be watching. Satan took away Abel's life through Cain. Cain was the first seed of woman. The devil tried to destroy every child that looked like a possible threat to him for around four thousand years; when he felt the greatest threat, Satan would influence an evil ruler to give a command to have the young children in that region murdered (Exodus 1:22, Matthew 2:16).

And the dragon stood before the woman which was ready to be delivered, for to devour her child as soon as it was born.
And she brought forth a man child, who was to rule all nations with a rod of iron: and her child was caught up unto God, and to his throne.
Revelation 12:4-5

Satan stood before the woman, looking for the "seed of woman" that God prophesied to him about for around four thousand years. The woman gave birth to a man child who was to rule all nations with a rod of iron. Jesus is the man child spoken of in verse 5. The woman's identity mentioned in Revelation 12:1 is Israel because of the twelve stars that were upon her crown. Jesus came from the seed or lineage of Israel. Israel had twelve sons. Jesus is the seed of woman for which the devil was looking to try to devour.

After Jesus died on the cross and rose from the dead, He revealed Himself to His disciples and many others for forty days. On the fortieth day, Jesus was raptured into heaven right before their eyes (Acts 1:3, 9). *"The man child was caught up to God, and to his throne."* The Bible also says in Ephesians 1:20 that *"God set Jesus at his own right hand in the heavenly places."* After Jesus was caught up to God, there was a war in heaven. Do you know why? Satan was angry he had just been whipped and made a mockery of by

Jesus. Satan thought he could enter into heaven just like he had done many times before and pick up where he had left off. He thought he would bring more accusations against God's people; but for the first time, Michael, the mighty warrior of God, stopped him at the entrance of heaven! Can you imagine what was going through Satan's mind? He had to be the most confused individual you had ever seen! Satan's legal right to enter into heaven had been denied!

The Power of the Blood

The war that is mentioned in Revelation 12:7 happened after Jesus was caught up to God's throne around two thousand years ago. And verse 8 says that *"Satan and his angels did not prevail, <u>neither was their place found any more in heaven</u>."* Satan can no longer come before God and accuse you or anyone else for that matter. Satan has not only been cast down, but he has also been cast out! He has been defeated and completely stripped of all the power that he had. Do you know why Satan is no longer allowed to go into heaven like he did on a regular basis before the cross? THE BLOOD!

Satan thought he had killed Jesus by "legal" means. He used the "religious" of that day, the people that knew what the scriptures and the law said, to crucify Jesus. But Satan forgot about one thing: THE BLOOD! Jesus was conceived by the Holy Spirit, which made His blood innocent. Not only that, Jesus was tempted in every way, but He was without sin. So Satan killed an innocent man, and this alone gave Jesus the right to go into the center of the earth to take the keys of both death and hell.

Jesus said in Matthew 28:18, *"All power is given unto me in heaven and in earth."* Jesus took from Satan what he (Satan) had received from Adam, and Jesus gave it back into our hands. This is why He said, *"Behold, I give unto you power to tread on serpents and scorpions, and over all the power of the enemy: and nothing shall by any means hurt you"* (Luke 10:19), and *"Whatsoever ye shall bind on earth shall be bound in heaven: and whatsoever ye shall loose on earth shall be loosed in heaven"* (Matthew 18:18). The very same power and authority that Adam had before he sinned was taken from the devil and given back to the body of Christ.

And they overcame him (Satan) by the blood of the Lamb, and by the word of their testimony; and they loved not their lives unto the death.

Revelation 12:11

Three things mentioned here that will give you the victory over Satan and anything he has to offer: (1) The Blood of Jesus, (2) The Spoken Word, and (3) Proper Focus. As a believer, you should apply the blood (not plead the blood), speak the Word of God with boldness and authority, and keep what is important ("they loved not their lives unto the death" - *"not in love with yourself"*, Message Bible) before your eyes. When you do this, you will have victory in everything; God's Word promises it.

Job did not have these promises like you do today. He was not only limited in his knowledge of God, but he was also limited in his knowledge concerning the devil and his tactics as well. When studying the Bible, you will find the name Satan mentioned in only fifteen verses in the Old Testament, and eleven of those fifteen verses are in the book of Job. When Jesus showed up, the first thing He did in His earthly ministry was cast out a devil in the local church (Mark 1:23). Everyone was stunned, and said, *"What thing is this? What new doctrine is this?"* This was completely new to everyone. Jesus revealed the goodness of God by setting people free from the devil's hands. He healed the sick, raised the dead, set the leper free, and it was through the ministry of Jesus that the devil's deception was unmasked and God's true nature was revealed.

Chapter 9

Paul's Thorn in the Flesh

Paul was definitely one of the most powerful witnesses for Jesus Christ that God has ever had. He wrote over half of the New Testament and followed God with a zeal and passion like no other, but Paul was not without error in his life. He was human just like you are, and he made mistakes during his walk with the Lord. Much like the previous chapter discussed about Job, most people quote only what they have heard concerning "the thorn in the flesh", but have never actually read about it for themselves. Let's take a close look at the scripture concerning this in its entirety:

And lest I should be exalted above measure through the abundance of the revelations, there was given to me a thorn in the flesh, the messenger of Satan to buffet me, lest I should be exalted above measure.

For this thing I besought the Lord thrice, that it might depart from me.

And he said unto me, My grace is sufficient for thee: for my strength is made perfect in weakness.

II Corinthians 12:7-9

<u>Messenger of Satan</u>

There is no place in this scripture where you will find

that God gave this thorn in the flesh to Paul. The Bible says,

"There was given to me a thorn in the flesh, the <u>messenger</u>

<u>of Satan</u>..." As we have previously discussed, God is not

interested in bringing, causing, or "allowing" anything that

is of a bad nature to come into any of His children's lives.

God loves us, and He wants the best for us all the time.

Paul was a powerful force for the kingdom of God, and

the devil was trying to attack him just like he was trying to

attack Peter and anyone else that caused him problems. The

thorn in the flesh was a demon spirit that was sent from the devil to try to destroy Paul. Since the demon was unable to kill Paul, he did what he could by stirring up all kinds of problems to come Paul's way so he would be hindered in promoting the gospel of Jesus. The thorn in the flesh came from Satan, not God!

God's Kingdom is not Divided!

But when the Pharisees heard it, they said, This fellow (Jesus) doth not cast out devils, but by Beelzebub the prince of the devils.

And Jesus knew their thoughts, and said unto them, Every kingdom divided against itself is brought to desolation; and every city or house divided against itself shall not stand:

And if Satan cast out Satan, he is divided against himself; how shall then his kingdom stand?

Matthew 12:24-26

I love what Jesus said to the religious crowd when they said He was casting out demons by using the devil himself: *"Every house divided against itself shall not stand."* In other words, Jesus was saying, *"I cannot use the devil to harm people, and at the same time, cast him out of people."* The same words are true concerning sickness and disease. Jesus will never place a sickness or a disease on someone and then heal him of it later. If He operated this way, His kingdom would be divided, and it would be unable to stand.

When you look in the gospels, you will see Jesus healing the sick, casting out devils, and raising the dead. Jesus came to destroy (undo) the works of the devil, and He is the same yesterday, today, and forever (Hebrews 13:8). There is no place in the scriptures where you will find Jesus putting sickness on someone or allowing a person to go through a trial or endure pain for a while. When people came to Him in faith, expecting to receive, they went away healed or whole every time.

A lot of people believe that God is either testing them or He is allowing the devil to test them when they are going through a trial, but James 1:13 says, *"Let no man say when he is tempted (tested), I am tempted of God: for God cannot be tempted with evil, neither tempteth he any man."* God has no interest in testing His children just as parents have no interest in testing their own children; if He did, His kingdom would not be able to stand because there would be division in His own house.

What Was the Thorn?

I have heard all kinds of ridiculous answers to this question, and most of those answers revolve around some kind of sickness or disease. Paul's thorn in the flesh was *not* a sickness or a disease at all. The Bible gives us answers to everything if we would just "read the lines" instead of reading "in-between the lines."

We already know that it was a messenger of Satan, and the Bible declares this demon was a thorn in the flesh. Have you ever had a splinter or thorn in your hand or foot? A thorn is nothing less than a nagging nuisance that causes pain. The Greek word for thorn is *skolops*, which means *point or prickle that causes annoyance.*

God told the children of Israel in Numbers 33:55, *"But if you will not drive out the inhabitants of the land from before you; then it shall come to pass, that those which ye let remain of them shall be <u>pricks</u> in your eyes, and <u>thorns</u> in your sides, and shall vex you in the land wherein ye dwell."* This is exactly what the demon spirit was doing to Paul; he was a vexing nuisance that caused problems everywhere Paul journeyed. This "harassing" spirit became a part of Paul's everyday life, but it didn't have to be that way at all.

Another important fact is this demon was sent by special assignment from Satan to "buffet" Paul. The word "buffet" means to *rap (beat) with a fist.* This demon was bringing blow after blow into Paul's life to try to stop him from doing the work of God. Let's look at the previous chapter to find out what kind of trouble this demon spirit was stirring up in Paul's life:

Of the Jews five times received I forty stripes save one.

Thrice was I beaten with rods, once was I stoned, thrice I suffered shipwreck, a night and a day I have been in the deep;

In journeyings often, in perils of waters, in perils of robbers, in perils by mine own countrymen, in perils by the heathen, in perils in the city, in perils in the wilderness, in perils in the sea, in perils among false brethren;

In Damascus the governor under Aretas the king kept the city of the Damascenes with a garrison, desirous to apprehend me:

And through a window in a basket was I let down by the wall, and escaped his hands.

II Corinthians 11:24-26, 32-33

Talk about a rough life! All of this mentioned in this scripture was a direct result of the messenger of Satan that was sent to buffet Paul. Everywhere Paul journeyed, this "harassing" spirit was stirring up problems. Satan was manipulating and deceiving people that did not have a love for God to try to destroy Paul.

Here is a good moment for a logical question: If Paul felt like God was behind all of his testing and trials, then why would he try to escape from the governor's hands? Wouldn't he just allow the "will of God" to be done in his life? This is likened to someone that comes down with a sickness and believes that God is allowing it in order to teach him something. If this was true, then the person that is sick should not call the doctor or take any medicine to try to get better. That person should just allow the "will of God" to be done in his life. Taking medicine or calling a doctor to get better would be fighting against God, wouldn't it? Do you see how dumb that is? Paul knew the "thorn in the flesh" wasn't from God, but he didn't activate the will of God through his faith. Paul did not command the "harassing" spirit to leave. In fact, it was Paul's own lack of knowledge (unbelief) that caused him to continuously go through those trials.

Someone might say, "But Brother Machen, God said in this world you will have tribulation!" I always respond with, "Have you read the rest of that verse?" It says, *"But be of good cheer, I (Jesus) have overcome the world"* (John 16:33). That tells me that no matter what the world may have to offer me, Jesus already overcame it; but it's up to me to activate His overcoming will in my life. It wasn't God's will for Paul to suffer all of those things, but like a lot of people, Paul had a "martyr's" mentality instead of the "overcomer's" mentality. God has accomplished everything He has ever needed to accomplish through His son Jesus. When He laid down His life on the cross, He overcame the devil. This is why Jesus said in John 19:30, *"It is finished!"* It is done! It is complete! The price for your sins, sicknesses, depression, sorrow, lack, and every other problem in this world has been paid for by the precious blood of Jesus. Now all you need to do is submit yourself to the provision that God has already finished (supplied) and resist the devil in the name of Jesus. Satan will have no choice but to flee from you.

Understanding Persecution

The Bible speaks about believers being persecuted, but it shouldn't affect you or cause harm in your life. Persecution comes for one reason: the Word of God (Mark 4:17). When the Word of God is planted in your heart, it will cause you to be right-standing (righteous) with God. When you become righteous, you will become a big problem for the enemy. This is why Jesus said in Matthew 5:10, *"Blessed are they which are persecuted for righteousness' sake: for theirs is the kingdom of heaven."* According to Luke 6:22, persecution refers to the things that people will speak about you. The Bible says they will hate you and separate you from their company because of the Word that is in your heart.

"But Pastor Machen, you don't know what so-in-so said about me!" You have much better things to do with your life than to worry and waste your time over what someone has said about you. In fact, if you would stop trying to defend yourself and instead would allow God to take care of that matter, you would be a much greater force for God's kingdom. He will take care of your business when you *"are about your Father's business"* (Luke 2:49).

Persecution will only affect you if you pay attention to it, and you should never take it personal either. Jesus will stand in the gap for you if you give Him allowance in your life. When He revealed Himself to Paul for the first time, He said, *"Saul, why are you persecuting ME?"* (Acts 9:4). Jesus takes it personal on your behalf! If someone is bringing false accusation against you because of your work for the Lord, leap for joy and rejoice as Luke 6:23 commands. This simply means you are right on track with God. In fact, if you are not being persecuted in this manner, you might want to check out your status with the kingdom of God (Luke 6:26).

If someone did try to harm you physically because of your passion for God, just lift up the shield of faith and walk in God's divine protection. Jesus did this many times in His life. When the angry, religious crowd tried to throw Him off of a cliff to stone Him at the beginning of His earthly ministry, God's provision made a way for Jesus to walk in-between them without being harmed (Luke 4:28-30).

When the army came to take Jesus away, He said to Peter, *"Thinkest thou that I cannot now pray to my Father, and he shall presently give me more than twelve legions of angels?"* (Matthew 26:53). God has not only given commandment for His angels to protect you, but He has also given you His personal armor. They exist for your complete protection in everything you do. In order to walk in God's protection though, you must activate it by your faith.

What Was the Answer?

My grace is sufficient for thee: for my strength is made perfect in weakness.
II Corinthians 12:9

Paul came to Jesus in prayer and asked Him three times for the demon to depart from him. Three times Jesus gave him the answer on how to deal with the "harassing" spirit that had an assignment from Satan. Let's establish two things that are extremely important: *Number One,* Jesus never said to Paul that he had to suffer with this problem, and *Number 2,* Jesus never said to him, "No, Paul." The old religious saying that God answers His people with yes, no, or maybe is an outright lie from the devil. My Bible tells me in II Corinthians 1:20, *"All the promises of God in him are YES and in him, Amen."* Jesus gave Paul exactly what he needed to take care of this demon: *"My grace is sufficient for you..."*

Looking at this with just face value, it may not mean much to you, but to Paul this meant everything. Before Paul became a Christian, his name was Saul of Tarsus, and he was not known for being a nice person. Saul was persecuting and killing new converts that proclaimed Jesus as the Savior and Son of God. One day when he was traveling on the road to Damascus, a light shined out of heaven and he heard a voice saying, *"Saul, Saul, why are you persecuting me?"* When Saul asked who was speaking, the voice answered, *"I am Jesus whom thou persecutest"* (Acts 9:5). Talk about God's grace! If anyone understood something about grace, it was definitely Paul.

Paul was a great candidate for God's grace to be revealed. He is the perfect example to show everyone that no one is excluded from God's love. Paul had a zeal for God, but it was not in agreement with the knowledge of God. Paul was persecuting and killing Christians, and he actually believed that he had the legal right under God's law to do this. Now we can understand why Paul spoke so much about grace in the gospels. He even said in I Corinthians 15:10, *"But by the grace of God I am what I am: and his grace which was bestowed upon me was not in vain; but I labored more abundantly than they all: yet not I, but the grace of God which was with me."* So what was it that saved Saul of Tarsus? What is it that saves you? The answer is God's grace, but it must be accepted and <u>activated by faith</u>. *"For by grace are ye saved through faith"* (Ephesians 2:8).

The word "grace" from the Greek means *favor, acceptance, and benefit.* Jesus said to Paul, *"My favor and acceptance is sufficient for you..."* Looking at the rest of this scripture and the meanings of each word really sheds light on the powerful answer that Jesus gave to Paul. Remember, Paul had been dealing with this demon spirit for some time. When Paul asked Jesus to do something about it, he was actually asking Jesus to do something that He had already given him the authority to overcome. Jesus already defeated Satan when He died on the cross and rose from the grave. When Jesus departed this earth, He gave His power and authority into the hands of His followers. This is one of the major problems in the body of Christ today; people are asking God to do something instead of commanding the devil to get off of their back like they're supposed to do!

Here is the breakdown of what Jesus said to Paul: *"My favor and acceptance* (grace) *is enough* (sufficient) *for you. My miraculous power* (strength) *is accomplished* (made perfect) *when you are ineffective in yourself* (in weakness)."

What Jesus was saying is this: "The same grace that saved you from your sins is the same grace that will save you from this demon spirit. I have given you the means to take care of this problem, now activate your deliverance through Me!"

What did Jesus do with demon spirits when He was in His earthly ministry? Matthew 8:16 says, *"He cast them out with His word."* There is no place in the Word of God where you will find Jesus asking God to do something about the devil. He always spoke with authority and commanded the devil and his demons to leave. Paul was operating in unbelief when he asked God to do something about the devil. Now he didn't wake up one morning and decide to intentionally operate in unbelief. Paul had simply forgotten about God's answer to his problem because of the strain of all the trials in his life. He lost sight of the truth that was able to make him free. This is why Paul later wrote, *"Therefore we ought to give the more earnest heed to the things which we have heard, lest at any time we should let them slip"* (Hebrews 2:1).

Paul's Stubbornness

The definition of the word "stubborn" in the dictionary means *unreasonable, often perversely unyielding; bull-headed.* In the scriptures, the meaning from the Hebrew has a little more punch to it: *to turn away, backsliding, rebellious, revolt.* In the Old Testament, there are a number of stories about how people allowed their own stubbornness to keep them from the plan of God. One of the most memorable accounts in the Bible is about Saul, the king of Israel, who refused to obey God's commandment concerning the Amalekites. God said to Saul in I Samuel 15:23, *"For rebellion is as the sin of witchcraft, and <u>stubbornness</u> is as iniquity and idolatry."* In the New Testament, there are also a number of examples of stubbornness, and Paul is definitely close to the top of the list.

The reason this is so important to discuss is because many Christians believe that Paul's suffering was due to God's plan in his life. The truth is, Paul brought many of the problems on himself through his own stubbornness and trying to do things his way instead of God's way. Please don't take the previous statement the wrong way; Paul was a tremendous witness for the Lord. Even when Paul was doing things within himself, God was able to use him, but Paul's own stubbornness brought the pain and hardships in his life. Three times God told Paul to do something, but he refused to obey God's voice. Let's take a look at this in the book of Acts; these scriptures will reveal how Paul refused God's provision:

And finding disciples (in the city of Tyre), we tarried there seven days: who said to Paul <u>through the Spirit</u>, that he should <u>not go up to Jerusalem</u>.
Acts 21:4

Would you agree with this scripture that the Holy Spirit spoke clearly to Paul through his fellow-disciples about danger in Jerusalem? At this point, the disciples were not speaking out of their emotions or by what they felt. They were led and instructed by the Holy Spirit to tell Paul to stay away from Jerusalem. I have heard Christians say this many times over the years, "I *felt* led by God to do so-and-so..." or "I *feel* led by the Holy Spirit to tell you thus-and-so..." As believers, we should never be moved by our feelings. Feelings and faith never mix, and "feeling led" is not scriptural. A Christian should never "feel led" about anything. You are either led by the Holy Spirit, or you are not led at all.

And as we tarried there many days, there came down from Judaea a certain prophet, named Agabus.

And when he was come unto us, he took Paul's girdle, and bound his own hands and feet, and said, <u>Thus saith the Holy Ghost</u>, So shall the Jews at Jerusalem bind the man that owneth this girdle, and shall deliver him into the hands of the Gentiles.

And when we heard these things, both we, and they of that place, besought him <u>not to go up to Jerusalem</u>.

Then Paul answered, What mean ye to weep and to break mine heart? For I am ready not to be bound only, but also to die at Jerusalem for the name of the Lord Jesus.

And when he would not be persuaded, we ceased, saying, The will of the Lord be done.

Acts 21:10-14

This is the second time God warned Paul concerning Jerusalem. It seems pretty straight forward to me, doesn't it to you? A prophet came to Paul and said, *"Thus says the Holy Ghost..."* This was not man's words. This was God's words trying to protect Paul, but he obviously did not want to hear what God had to say to him. Not only was Paul stubborn against the provision of God, but he also brought into existence his own bondage and his own death by the words of his mouth (verse 13). When you speak things that don't line up with the Word of God like Paul did, you will open yourself up to the devil's attack.

When the disciples heard the prophet speak this to Paul, they begged him to stay away from Jerusalem. When Paul wouldn't be persuaded, the disciples did like a lot of religious-minded people have done; they said, *"The will of the Lord be done."* According to the scriptures, the will of God was for Paul to stay away from Jerusalem. So when the disciples made that statement, it was out of emotion and ignorance of the Word of God. Just because something happens in this world doesn't mean it should be classified as the "will of God." A real friend to Paul should have said something like, "Now listen Paul, God is instructing you to stay away from Jerusalem, so straighten up and be obedient to what He has commanded you to do. And if you refuse to obey God, you will be in rebellion, and I am not going to be a part of it!"

The will of God is easy to know and it is in plain sight in the Bible. People that say things like, "Well, it must not have been God's will for that person to get healed" are speaking out of a religious and unbelieving mindset. God's will is for everyone to be healed just like it is His will for everyone to be saved. God's will for Paul was clear and concise, but he chose to do things his own way. God will never violate the free will that He has given you. In other words, God will never make you do anything. Everyone has a choice, and Paul chose to go to Jerusalem against the will of God. In reality, Paul chose bondage, torment, and ultimately his own death over the provision of God. God told him the proper choice to make because He wanted to protect him from harm. God was still able to use him mightily, but imagine what greater impact Paul would have made had he been obedient to the Lord in everything.

And it came to pass, that, when I was come again to Jerusalem, even while I prayed in the temple, I was in a trance;
And saw him saying unto me, <u>Make haste, and get thee quickly out of Jerusalem:</u> for they will not receive thy testimony concerning me.
And I said, Lord, they know that I imprisoned and beat in every synagogue them that believed on thee:
And when the blood of thy martyr Stephen was shed, I also was standing by, and consenting unto his death, and kept the raiment of them that slew him.
And he said unto me, <u>Depart: for I will send thee far hence unto the Gentiles.</u>

Acts 22:17-21

This is the third and final time that God warned Paul, and by this time Paul was already in Jerusalem. When Paul was praying, Jesus revealed Himself to him in a vision saying, *"Hurry, get out of Jerusalem!"* The response that

Paul gave to Jesus reveals to us why he was stubborn and rebellious toward God. Paul had un-forgiveness in his heart toward <u>himself</u> at this point in time in his ministry. Paul mentioned that he had persecuted the church and consented unto Stephen's death when Stephen was stoned. Notice that Jesus made no comment about this in His return statement to Paul. Do you know why? As far as Jesus was concerned, everything that Paul had done in the past was forgiven and washed away by the blood when Paul became born-again. Have you ever brought up your past to God when you were praying? Have you noticed that Jesus never talked to you about your forgiven past either?

Paul's own un-forgiveness kept him from receiving from God. Anytime a believer refuses to forgive himself or anyone else for that matter, he is operating in unbelief concerning God's grace and love that has been freely given through His blood. Fortunately, Paul did come to the knowledge of the truth. Later in his ministry, Paul wrote,

"Old things are passed away; behold all things are become new" (II Corinthians 5:17). He also wrote to the church at Philippi, *"This one thing I do, forgetting those things which are behind, and reaching forth unto those things which are before..."* (Philippians 3:13). Paul eventually learned how to forgive himself of the terrible things he had done before he was saved, but this was after he disobeyed God and had gone through many hardships. I wonder how many believers have gone through trials and hardships because of disobedience and un-forgiveness in their hearts.

Chapter 10

Understanding the Prayer of Faith

Is any among you afflicted? Let him pray. Is any merry? Let him sing psalms.

Is any sick among you? Let him call for the elders of the church; and let them pray over him, anointing him with oil in the name of the Lord:

And the prayer of faith shall save the sick, and the Lord shall raise him up; and if he have committed sins, they shall be forgiven him.

Confess your faults one to another, and pray one for another, that ye may be healed. The effectual fervent prayer of a righteous man availeth much.

James 5:13-16

I was reading this scripture one day, and the Holy Spirit asked me, "Why pray?" I said, "To change things?" He then said to me, "Exactly. That's what prayer does. It changes things." Let me ask you a couple of logical questions: If you are afflicted and there is no hope for deliverance, then why waste your time and pray? If you are sick and you believe that it is "God's will" for you to remain sick, then why pray to be healed? The Bible doesn't say to pray for the sick and then wait to see if it's God's will to heal them. The Bible doesn't say the prayer of faith "might" save the sick either. James 5:15 says, *"The prayer of faith SHALL (will) save the sick."* If you are afflicted or sick, when is the best time for you to receive deliverance? Does *Right Now* sound like a good time? Do you realize that we serve a "Right Now" God? Jesus performed instantaneous miracles because He had instantaneous faith and a perfect relationship with His Heavenly Father. We can also receive instantaneous miracles from God when we learn to pray with faith, believing what He has spoken. Prayer changes things, and learning how to pray in agreement with the Word is the only way to receive from God.

Prayer should be a priority in every believer's life, and understanding prayer and how it works is vital to overcoming the wicked one. The devil has blinded the eyes of many of God's children concerning prayer. Many Christians do not receive answers to their prayers and there are many reasons for this, but the two most common reasons are: *One,* they do not know how to pray, and *Two,* they are praying in unbelief. There are actually five different kinds of prayer mentioned in the Bible: 1. *Prayer of Faith,* 2. *Prayer of Petition or Request* (I John 5:15, Psalm 37:4), 3. *Prayer of Intercession* (Romans 8:27), 4. *Prayer of Wisdom or Guidance* (James 1:5), and 5. *Praying in the Spirit or Tongues* (Jude 1:20). All five of these prayers should be a normal part of a Christian's life, but the prayer of faith should be the most commonly used.

What is the Prayer of Faith?

The Holy Spirit gave me the definition of the prayer of faith in 1996. It is *a commanding voice that activates the will of God.* As recorded in the gospels, Jesus used this type of prayer in better than ninety percent of His ministry. Jesus cast out devils, healed the sick, made the blind to see, calmed the winds and the waves, and even raised the dead back to life with the prayer of faith. He did not ask God to do anything for Him when using this prayer. He commanded it!

Before you can command the will of God to be done, you must first know what the will of God is and believe it. The only way you can know the will of God is by drawing close to Him through meditating in His Word (God's will) every day and night. It would be impossible for you to command sickness to leave someone's body if you did not fully believe that it is God's will for everyone to be healed. Jesus knew the will of God, and He put it into action through the prayer of faith everywhere He went.

And Jesus stood over her (Peter's mother-in-law), and rebuked the fever; and it left her: and immediately she arose and ministered unto them.

Luke 4:39

Jesus had immediate results because He had immediate faith. He believed and expected God's will to be done. Jesus spoke to the fever and rebuked it with authority. The word "rebuke" means to *tax upon, to censure, or to forbid*. This was the prayer of faith in action. Jesus did *not* ask God to take the fever from Peter's mother-in-law. He simply spoke to the thing that was causing weakness in her body and it left her immediately.

Broken Arm Healed

My wife and I have two sons, and we have always spoken the Word of God over them concerning their healing and their protection. One Sunday evening after a church service, my oldest son was playing with some of his friends. He was six years old at the time. While running, he fell awkwardly, breaking one of the bones in his right forearm. I remember him running to his mother and me. He was crying and in terrible pain. There was no need to take him to a doctor to confirm what I already knew in the natural. We could see with our physical eyes that a bone had been broken in his arm, but we refused to accept this for our son.

We calmly walked him to the car and put him in the back seat. We shut his door, and then Andrea and I sat down in the front seat of the car. When seated, we both turned around placing our hands on his arm, and I said out loud, "Arm, you line up with the Word of God right now in Jesus' Name! Caleb, the Bible says in Psalm 34:20 that none of your bones will be broken, and that is what we receive for you in the Name of Jesus!" The moment we spoke this to Caleb and his arm, he immediately stopped crying. We not only physically felt the glory of God in our car, but we also felt the broken bone completely heal right under our hands as we prayed. I looked at Caleb and said, "Well?" He answered, "All better. Thanks Mom. Thanks Dad!"

We did not ask God to heal our son's arm; instead, we commanded the will of God to be done in his life. We used the prayer of faith, which is *a commanding voice that activates the will of God*. We didn't stop and ask God if it was His will for our son to be healed. We knew that anything that causes pain or harm comes from one source - the devil. We also knew that we had authority over him through the name of Jesus. We put into action the promise that had already been written in Psalm 34:20 concerning his bones, and we received a miracle. We have seen all kinds of miracles over the years: cancers completely dissolved, diabetes reversed, enlarged heart made whole, deaf ears opened, deliverance from migraine headaches, eyesight restored, just to name a few, all because of the prayer of faith.

I have had people ask me my thoughts concerning doctors. I have told them, "Doctors are fighting the same devil you are, but they have limited knowledge. I would also much rather trust in the one that created my body to keep it well, instead of trusting someone that is 'practicing' medicine." If Christians would learn to trust God for what He says (what has been written) instead of what their personal doctor, lawyer, or banker has to say, then there would be nothing lacking or missing in their lives.

Stop Waiting and Start Acting

If you are "waiting" on God to move in your life, you will unfortunately be waiting for a while. Faith doesn't "wait" on God. Faith will actually move God's power and anointing on your behalf. The woman that touched the hem of Jesus' garment activated her miracle by going to Him. The man that was let down through the roof where Jesus was preaching was healed because of his friends persistence. Blind Bartimaeus received his sight because he refused to be denied by the disciples when they told him to be quiet. In all three of these examples, their faith put a demand on God's anointing. In the first and last example, Jesus actually said to them, *"Your faith has made you whole"* (Mark 5:34, Mark 10:52). They did not "wait" on God to come and save them. They were not on Jesus' agenda when He woke up that morning; Jesus was on their agenda.

We have way too many "praying" Christians instead of "acting" Christians. Please don't misunderstand me. I definitely believe that prayer is important and I know we should learn to pray just like the Bible says; however, if you are always in your "prayer closet" asking God to do something that He has already done, then you are praying in unbelief. This is why Paul was having a hard time receiving from God when he went to Him concerning the "thorn in the flesh." Paul was asking God to do something concerning the devil that He had already given him the authority to resist through His name. When the name of Jesus is activated properly through faith, Satan and every demon that exists in this world must come under complete submission to the Word of God (Phil. 2:9, Luke 10:17).

In I Samuel 17, there is a story about David who was sent by his father to take some food to his brothers who were in a battle with the Philistines in the valley of Elah. When David arrived, the Philistine champion (Goliath) came and presented himself like he had been doing the previous forty days. Goliath challenged the Israelites to send a warrior to fight with him. Everyone ran in fear except for David. David was taken before King Saul, and when Saul heard David speak of what he was going to do to that giant, he sent him with confidence to fight Goliath. The interesting thing about this story is David never prayed about going to fight Goliath; it's not in the Bible at all. Here is the point: David knew that Goliath stood against his covenant with God, and he wasn't required to pray about something that he already had the answer for. The same thing holds true for believers today: sickness, debt, pain, cares, hardship, worry, trouble, etc. all stand against God's covenant promises. You should not pray about any of these things; instead, do something about them. Too many times, believers are praying *about* their problems when they should be speaking *directly to* them.

Here is another important fact concerning David when he went out to face the giant: the Bible says he ran toward Goliath with one stone in his sling. Talk about confidence! He ran because he knew the only outcome was victory. He had complete faith and confidence in his God with absolutely no place given to unbelief. In fact, I Samuel 17:40 says that David chose five smooth stones and placed them in his bag before fighting Goliath. Do you know why he chose five stones? Goliath had four brothers and it was customary in that time that if a brother was killed in battle, the remaining brother(s) would avenge his death. David was prepared to kill all four of Goliath's brothers. David had one stone per giant!

Command Ye Me

Thus saith the Lord, the Holy One of Israel, and his Maker, Ask me of things to come concerning my sons, and concerning the work of my hands, command ye me.
Isaiah 45:11

There are two kinds of prayer mentioned in this scripture. The first one mentioned is the prayer of wisdom (*ask me of things to come*), and the second one mentioned is the prayer of faith (*command ye me*). Many Christians are asking the Lord to do things for them instead of commanding them to be done. This is another reason they do not receive from God. To understand what to ask for and what to command, you must determine what the work of God's hand applies to (*concerning the work of my hands...*). A hand represents action and authority in the Bible. Here is an easy way to look at it: if something needs to be done, you should use the prayer of faith (command it to be done), and if guidance is needed, you should use the prayer of wisdom (ask God for direction).

When Jesus spoke to the winds and the waves, He used the prayer of faith. When He healed the sick and cast out demons, He used the prayer of faith. When He raised the dead back to life, He used the prayer of faith. When He spoke to the fig tree, He used the prayer of faith. Jesus commanded things that were physical in nature to obey a spiritual law. Jesus only asked His Heavenly Father for something when He needed guidance; everything else, He commanded.

Take a closer look at James 5:14: *"Is any sick among you? Let him call for the elders of the church..."* As the pastor of World Victory Church, I receive a lot of phone calls from members of the church, and many of those calls are requests for prayer concerning healing for their bodies. I have noted over the years that over seventy-five percent of the calls that have requested prayer for healing have come after they have been to the doctor or after they have made an appointment to go to the doctor. The Bible says to call for the elders of the church and allow them to put the prayer of faith into action to eliminate the sickness. There is no "Plan B" with God. Too often, believers have had more faith in what the natural world says than in what the Bible says; this is called unbelief.

I am not against doctors by any means. Medical technology has improved tremendously over the years, and I believe that many people in the medical profession are working hard to fight against the diseases of this world, but they don't come anywhere close to what the prayer of faith will do. With a doctor's visit, a person has to take off work, wait in line, and pay money for the whole process hoping for a good outcome. With The Great Physician, you stay at work, receive immediately, and the price is free because it was paid for at Calvary!

The church should be a place of healing, peace, and power. Every leader in a church should know how to activate the prayer of faith. In times past, I have had different members of our praise team call me on a Sunday morning saying, "Pastor, I'm sorry for the late notice, but I'm not feeling well, and I will not make it to the service today." My response has always been the same: "Come to church acting in faith, and by the time you get here, your body will line up according to the Word." I can honestly say that most of them took my challenge, and God manifested His healing in their bodies because of their faith and corresponding actions. If they were still feeling bad when they arrived, I took a personal moment to use the prayer of faith to rebuke the ailment just like Jesus did, and God's healing manifested every time.

<u>Calling Things into Existence</u>

Another powerful aspect concerning the prayer of faith is found in Romans 4:17; it says, *"God calleth those things which be not as though they were."* In other words, God called into existence something that did not exist before. In the book of Genesis, God used this principle when He created the world. Genesis 1:3 says, *"And God said, Let there be light: and there was light."* God commanded light to come into existence with the words of His mouth; He was calling things that did not exist as though they did exist. Darkness covered the whole earth before God said, *"Let there be light."* It is important to know that God did not speak about the darkness at all. He spoke into existence what He desired to have, and He gave no acknowledgement of the darkness that existed in the natural.

God did the same thing when He changed Abram's name to Abraham. Abram had already been given the promise from God that he would have a promise seed, but Abram was having a hard time seeing it in his spirit man. Abram said to God in Genesis 15:2, *"What wilt thou give me, SEEING I go childless...?"* Abram had an inner image problem concerning God's promise. Many Christians have this very same problem. You must see it on the inside before you can produce it on the outside. Concerning Abram's promise, God had to help him by changing his name from Abram to Abraham. The name "Abraham" means *father of many nations.* The Bible says Abram was ninety-nine years old when God changed his name to Abraham, and he was one hundred years old when Sarah gave birth to Isaac (Genesis 17:1-5, 21:5). How long does it take to produce a child in this natural world? When you do the math, you will see that when God speaks, things change. Here is something to ponder on: if you are a Christian, you are made in God's image; therefore when you speak, things should change also. The question is, what kind of words are coming out of your mouth? Your words will produce life or death, freedom or bondage, health or sickness, prosperity or debt, etc. You choose what you say, and what you say is what you will have!

In the New Testament, Jesus called things that did not exist as though they did exist when He approached someone that had just recently passed away. Concerning the daughter of Jairus, Jesus said, *"The damsel is not dead, but sleepeth"* (Mark 5:39). When He said this, the people that were close to the family laughed at Him and ridiculed the very thought of Him making such a statement. After casting out everyone that had unbelief from within the house, Jesus allowed only Peter, James, and John along with the father and the mother of the girl to enter. Jesus then reached down and took the little girl by the hand saying, *"Damsel, I say unto you, Arise!"* Jesus commanded her to come back to life, and she obeyed Him. When He said, *"She sleepeth"*, Jesus was calling into existence the desired end result.

Jesus did the same thing concerning Lazarus in John 11:11. He said to His disciples, *"Our friend Lazarus sleepeth; but I go, that I may awake him out of sleep."* The disciples did not understand that Jesus was actually speaking of Lazarus' death, so John 11:14 declares, *"Then said Jesus unto them plainly, Lazarus is dead."* It's important to understand the only reason Jesus said this was because of His disciples. They were definitely not the brightest people in the world! Even after Jesus plainly said to them that Lazarus was dead, Thomas said, *"Let us also go, that we may die with him"* (verse 16). Talk about warped thinking! This is what Jesus had to deal with every day for three and a half years. Now we can have a much better understanding of why

Jesus said several times to His disciples, *"How long am I going to be with you?"*

The original statement that Jesus made to His disciples was, *"Lazarus is asleep."* The fact was (reality in the natural), Lazarus was actually dead, <u>but truth is always greater than fact.</u> Jesus was speaking truth over fact when He said, *"Lazarus is asleep."* He was activating a spiritual law over a natural law. John 8:32 says, *"Ye shall know the truth, and the truth shall make you free."* Most people only know facts, and that is what they mix their faith and actions with; but when you know the real truth, God's power will make you free in everything. Look at it this way: if your body is sick, the sickness may be a fact, but the truth is *"By His stripes, you are healed"* (I Peter 2:24). So you have a choice: you can either speak what you see in the natural (fact) or you can speak what you see in the Bible (truth). Someone might say, "If I say I am healed when I am actually sick, then that would be called a lie." Jesus obviously didn't see it that way, and we need to learn to renew our minds to think like He thinks. You are not denying that sickness exists; you are simply denying its right to exist in your body.

When Jesus came to the grave where Lazarus was buried, He lifted His eyes to heaven and prayed to God. Besides the prayer that Jesus prayed right before He went to the cross, this prayer in John 11:41-42 is actually one of the longest prayers that Jesus prayed that is recorded in the Bible. What Jesus said in this prayer is astounding:

> **Father, I thank thee that thou hast heard me.**
> **And I know that thou hearest me always: but because of the people which stand by, <u>I said it</u>, that they may believe that thou hast sent me.**
>
> *John 11:41-42*

What was Jesus talking about when He said to God, *"But because of the people which stand by, <u>I said it</u>."*? The answer is when Jesus plainly said, *"Lazarus is dead."* Jesus spoke in the natural (*spoke unto them plainly*) that Lazarus was dead because of the disciples that stood by Him. Before He raised Lazarus from the grave, He made sure that God under-stood exactly why He said *"Lazarus is dead"* to the disci-ples. Jesus was basically "making good" with His Heavenly Father. Do you get it? Speaking something negative or in the natural was not just unusual or uncommon to Jesus, it was wrong! Jesus considered it to be sin. God hears everything we say, and it's the words that proceed from our own mouth that either condemn or justify a situation in our lives. You cannot expect good results if you speak what you see in the natural and at the same time pray or speak what the Word of God says. The Bible calls this being double minded (unbe-lief). Unfortunately, it is impossible to receive from God if you are operating in this manner (James 1:7-8).

What You Pray is Vitally Important

After praying to God about what He said to His disciples, Jesus said with a loud voice, *"Lazarus, come forth"* (John 11:43). This is another example of the prayer of faith. Jesus was the commanding voice that activated the will of God concerning Lazarus. Notice that Jesus did not pray a long prayer to God, and He did not ask God to raise Lazarus from the dead. The power of God was within Jesus to get the job done, but He had to activate it by commanding the *"work of God's hand."* According to Romans 8:11, this very same power resides on the inside of every born-again believer.

When God calls someone, He also equips him. He tells us in John 14:12 that if we believe in Him, we would not only do the works (miracles) He did, but we would also do greater works than what Jesus did. First, it would be impossible for us to do anything within ourselves. Here is a great revelation: *in yourself*, you can do nothing (no, not one thing). Second, it would be impossible to do His works or even greater works unless you have been equipped with the means or ability to do them. So, in yourself you can do nothing, but *in Christ*, you can do all things because He gives you the strength (power) to do them (Philippians 4:13).

What you pray is vitally important in releasing this awe-some power from God. I have heard some real interesting prayers over the years, especially when I have been in meetings with other pastors. You can know a lot about people and their walk with God by what comes out of their mouth, especially when they pray. Have you ever heard someone use the "Thee's" and "Thou's" when he is praying? Or how about the prayer that never ends? It may be humorous, but you know exactly what I am saying. I have also heard some real nice, eloquent prayers, but they didn't do anything for the glory of God. The truth is, God never even hears a prayer that is full of "fluff"; it never reaches heaven. Any prayer that is not faith-filled or doesn't line up with the Word of God is just empty, useless words.

Jesus did not pray long prayers in public when He was here on the earth, so why should we think that He hears our long, whining prayers? The Word of God instructs us to draw close to God by getting in our "prayer closest" in secret, and when we come out, we will be able to manifest God's presence to everyone we come in contact within this world (Matthew 6:6). Most people view prayer as their last effort to receive God's help to deliver them from their present trouble. Praying in faith and in agreement with the Word of God will definitely save anyone from his present afflictions, but the real meaning of prayer is communication with the Heavenly Father. When you understand this, you will never again need to go to God to save you out of your problems; instead, His guidance and counsel through prayer will keep you from ever having problems in the first place.

Unbelieving Prayers

Many Christians are praying in unbelief. God wants to bless His people, and He is definitely interested in answering prayer, but He has to hear the prayer first to be able to answer it. If you do not pray in faith and in complete agreement with His Word, then your prayer is full of unbelief. God does not hear unbelieving prayers. God hears only faith-filled prayers. Here is an example of an unbelieving prayer: "Lord, just do whatever it takes to save so-in-so." This is a prayer of unbelief because God has already done everything He ever needed to do for that person through His son Jesus. Praying for the Holy Spirit to send forth laborers from God to come across that person's path to witness to him would be a more appropriate faith-filled prayer (Matt. 9:38). Here is another example: "Lord, if it is your will, heal so-in-so." This is also a prayer of unbelief, because it is God's will to heal everyone, just like it is His will to save everyone. A Christian does not have the right to pray, "If it be Thy will..." Instead, he should find out what the will of God is by reading the Bible. Once he does this, he will be able to activate what is written by speaking it through the prayer of faith. This is exactly how Jesus overcame Satan when he came to tempt Him in the wilderness. He spoke out loud to Satan, *"It is written..."*

Every time you pray in agreement with God's covenant promises, you should expect to receive exactly for what you are praying. Faith does not hope or wish; it believes and expects. It's not the eloquence or length of a prayer that matters; it's the content. And if you do not know exactly what to pray concerning a certain situation, then find a scripture that applies to that problem, and pray that scripture over it.

Details are also very important in your prayers. James 4:3 says, *"Ye ask, and receive not, because ye ask amiss..."* Specific prayers bring specific answers. God's people should not be afraid of the devil hearing their prayers. The only power Satan will ever have in a believer's life is the power that he gives to him. I pray out loud so the devil can hear me! There is nothing in the Bible about "unspoken" prayer requests either. If it is unspoken, it will go unheard, and therefore it will be unanswered.

When you learn to pray the way God intended you to pray, you will be able to pray like Elijah prayed. Elijah was flesh and blood just like you are. When he prayed, there was no rain for three and a half years; when he prayed again, the heavens opened up and brought forth rain. This is what the Bible means when it says, *"The effectual fervent prayer of a righteous man availeth (accomplishes) much"* (James 5:16).

Chapter 11

You Can Move Mountains

And Jesus answering saith unto them, Have faith in God.

For verily I say unto you, That whosoever shall say unto this mountain, Be thou removed, and be thou cast into the sea; and shall not doubt in his heart, but shall believe that those things which he saith shall come to pass; he shall have whatsoever he saith.

Mark 11:22-23

Based on what Jesus said, moving a mountain is much easier than what most people have thought. I have heard some preachers say that Jesus was talking about moving a "spiritual" mountain instead of a "real", physical mountain. Without any doubt, this was a "real" mountain Jesus was referring to because He had just commanded a "real" fig tree to dry up from the roots. I have become tickled at times when religious people try to explain away the miraculous power of God. One time, I heard a theologian explaining how Moses and the children of Israel were able to cross the Red Sea. He said they were actually able to cross the sea because they went to the other side through a shallow part that was only one to two feet deep. If that was true, that means that God was able to do a bigger miracle than just divide the sea on both sides. He caused Pharaoh and the Egyptians to all drown in two feet of water! I think it's time to believe what the Bible says, don't you?

Moving a mountain starts with having faith in God. A better translation of Mark 11:22 is, *"Have the faith of God."* Someone might say, "I could never have faith like that!" But in order to move a real mountain, a person would need the faith of God or *"God's kind of faith."* According to Romans 12:3, every Christian has been given the same measure of faith, but you are personally responsible for your own increase of faith. Think of your faith like a muscle. Your natural muscles can only increase in strength and size if they are exercised. This is why when the disciples said, *"Lord, increase our faith"*, Jesus said, *"If ye had faith as a grain of mustard seed, ye might say unto this sycamine tree, Be thou plucked up by the root and be thou planted in the sea; and it should obey you"* (Luke 17:5-6). Jesus told His disciples the only way to increase their faith was by exercising or putting into action what they had already been given. The most common way to activate your faith is by speaking faith-filled words out of your mouth. Did you know there are only two things recorded in the Bible at which Jesus marveled? They are faith and unbelief (Matthew 8:10, Mark 6:6), and both were manifested by the words that people spoke.

The Value God Has Placed on Your Words

Through faith we understand that the worlds were framed by the word of God, so that things which are seen were not made by things which do appear.
Hebrews 11:3

God created the world and everything in it by words. They were made or framed by the words that proceeded from His mouth. The phrase, *"And God said,"* is mentioned ten times in the first chapter of the book of Genesis. This means that the basic makeup of everything that can be seen with the natural eye is words. Even though words cannot be seen with the physical eye, it is the very thing that created the universe, and it (the spoken word) is the spiritual law that God has ordained this natural world to abide under. When Jesus told His disciples to speak to the sycamine tree and to the mountain, He said they would literally obey them. Here is the reason why: the sycamine tree and the mountain are both natural things that were created by words, and they only exist because of a spiritual law. So if someone speaks faith-filled words to a natural thing, the natural law will have no choice but to submit to the very thing that created it. In reality, words would be moving the basic and fundamental part of a mountain or tree - words! Furthermore, this power is available for every born-again Christian.

Now we can better understand why the earth stopped rotating when Joshua commanded the sun and the moon to be still. Words created the sun, the moon, and the earth. When Joshua spoke with only the faith of God in his heart, the earth had no choice but to stop rotating on its axis. Jesus also spoke to the winds, the waves, and the fig tree. These were all physical things that were created by a spiritual law. Matthew 8:16 says, *"Jesus cast out demon spirits with his word and healed all that were sick."* In the same likeness, if a believer has a sickness and would speak to the ailment with faith-filled words through the name of Jesus, the physical sickness would have to bow its knee. Speaking the name of Jesus is important to every born-again believer. His name is above every name that is named here on the earth (Philippians 2:9). If you speak His name with authority and faith, nothing will be impossible! Cancer, Arthritis, Osteoporosis, Heart

Disease, etc. are all names that must submit to the name of Jesus. The only way you will see the glory of God move in your life is by activating His name with *"God's kind of faith."*

Every word you speak is filled with power. This is a spiritual law that God placed in action in the very beginning. This law works for both believers and non-believers. According to Proverbs 18:21, *"Death and life are in the power of the tongue: and they that love it shall eat the fruit thereof."* Power is in every word you speak whether you believe in it or not; however, as previously discussed in chapter four, when a believer yields himself to this understanding, he will be able to benefit from this power. In other words, a person could pray all day long for someone, but if he doesn't believe that his words (prayers) are with power, nothing will happen.

There is a story of seven sons of Sceva that tried to cast out a demon because they had heard that Paul was casting out demons through the name of Jesus. Acts 19:13 tells us that the seven sons said to the demon, *"We adjure you by Jesus whom Paul preacheth."* The demon mocked them, saying, *"Jesus I know, and Paul I know; but who are you?"* The demon that was in that person leaped on all seven young men to where they fled from the house naked and wounded. They did not know Jesus personally and they were only "trying" what they had heard someone else do. They spoke something, but they didn't believe in what they were saying. This is not something you try. This is something you do!

The other thing I like about this scripture in Acts 19 is that the demon recognized Jesus and Paul in the same sentence: *"Jesus I know, and Paul I know..."* Paul's name had reached Satan's headquarters and his name was placed on a priority list. He was causing all kinds of problems for the devil. He was casting out demons, healing the sick, and even raising the dead. Sound familiar? Paul was recognized in the same category as Jesus Himself! I want to be on the devil's top five "Most Wanted" list, don't you? If you are at the top of Satan's list, that means you are on heaven's top five "Most

Used by God" list.

**Whosoever shall say unto this mountain… and shall
not doubt in his heart, but shall believe that those things
which he saith shall come to pass; he shall have whatsoever he saith.**

Mark 11:23

If people really believed that every word they speak

is full of power, they probably wouldn't say over ninety

percent of the things they have been saying. In my house,

we don't speak sickness, pain, or problems. We don't talk

about things that are connected to the system of this world

or death. We don't even jest or joke around with our words.

My wife and I have learned to say what we mean and mean

what we say. Jesus said in Matthew 5:37, *"Let your commu-

nication be, Yea, yea; Nay, nay: for whatsoever is more than

these cometh of evil."* Any word that doesn't line up with

the Word of God is a word of unbelief, and I refuse to allow

it in my life.

I don't even say things like, "That tickles me to death", or "That drives me up the wall", or "My feet are killing me", etc. Think about it: all of these previous statements are lies, and if a Christian speaks something that has no truth to it, he will deceive his own heart. He will be unable to benefit from the revelation in Proverbs 18:21 because he doesn't believe his own words are with power. If he believed every word he spoke would come to pass, he would never say things like, "That tickles me to death", etc. This is why the psalmist prayed this prayer in Psalm 141:3: *"Set a watch (guard), O Lord, before my mouth; keep the door of my lips."* Believers shouldn't walk or talk like the world. Someone might ask, "Is it really that important?" According to God it is, and if you learn to place the same value on your words like He does, then you can be just like Samuel. The Bible says as he grew in the Lord, none of the words that came out of his mouth ever fell to the ground void of power (I Samuel 3:19).

<u>Nothing is Impossible</u>

Believing (having faith) is the key to receiving from God. The following scriptures give a powerful insight on how to make things that seem impossible become a reality:

For with God all things are possible.

Mark 10:27

If thou canst believe, all things are possible to him that believeth.

Mark 9:23

Most Christians have no problem in believing that all things are possible to God. After all, He is God, The Almighty, The Creator of the universe! But when it comes to the latter scripture, they have a difficult time believing this could ever apply to them. Satan is constantly trying to convince believers that they are unworthy and powerless to receive from God. Here is the reality: the very same power that raised Christ from the dead actually dwells in every born-again believer (Romans 8:11). The only thing that would keep a Christian from receiving from God is if he did not believe what God has spoken; this is called unbelief.

Jesus said in Mark 16:17-18, *"And these signs shall follow them that <u>believe</u>; In my name shall they cast out devils... they shall lay hands on the sick, and they shall recover."* The signs that Jesus speaks of will only follow people who actually believe that the signs will follow them. There is no place in the Bible that says these signs passed away with the apostles. It says, *"These signs shall follow <u>them that believe</u>..."* Remember this is a "whosoever" gospel. If you believe this scripture has your name on it, your actions would agree with what you believe. You would be willing to pray for the sick, cast out devils, and do anything that God asked or commanded you to do. Most people do not believe they are capable of praying for the sick or casting out a demon. Their own unbelief keeps them from doing a mighty work for the Lord.

Your Actions Reveal What You Believe

Even so faith, if it hath not works [corresponding actions], **is dead, being alone.**

James 2:17, brackets mine

Faith cannot produce by itself. It must have corresponding actions to produce a harvest in your life. The woman with the issue of blood (Mark 5) did not receive her miracle until her actions lined up with what she said. Naaman, the leper, as recorded in II Kings 5, did not receive his miracle until he acted in faith on what Elisha instructed him to do. One of my favorite stories in the Bible is when Jesus performed His first miracle by turning water into wine. This was the very first miracle that Jesus performed here on the earth, and it was a miracle of "luxury" rather than a miracle of need. John 2:5 says, *"His mother saith unto the servants, Whatsoever he saith unto you, do it."* There would have been no miracle if the servants chose not to place action with what was spoken.

Whatever God tells you, just do it! Your miracle depends upon it.

You can tell what someone believes by how they act. Many people believe that God will perform in their life in His timing or someday in the future. Their words and their actions will line up with what they believe, and their actions produce the harvests. As a result, their miracles in life will always be sometime in the future because that is exactly what they believe in their heart. Let me put it another way: if a Christian gets sick, it is easy to see what he believes by what his first action is. If he calls the doctor, then his action shows he believes the doctor has the answer for the illness. If he calls the elders of the church according to James 5, then his action reveals that he believes the answer comes through the power of prayer.

In most cases, the first action in any given situation is not necessarily what you do, but what you say. This is why Jesus turned to Jairus and said, *"Don't be afraid, only believe."*

If Jairus would have changed his original words spoken to Jesus (*Come lay your hands on my daughter, and she shall be healed*) and said something in unbelief, Jesus would have been unable to raise his daughter from the dead. Jesus was helping Jairus keep his words in line so Jairus could receive his miracle. If Jarius would have said something in unbelief, he would have been double minded. James 1:7 says, *"Let not that man think that he shall receive any thing of the Lord."* If the devil is trying to put sickness on your body, simply refuse to speak things like, "I don't feel good", or "I'm sick." Instead, your first action should be to speak the Word of God with authority, and command the sickness to get away from you. Now if you really believed that God has healed your body, then you wouldn't lie around in bed acting like you were sick. *"Faith without works is dead, being alone"* (James 2:17).

My wife was playing in a softball game a few years back and twisted her knee as she slid into second base. It was evident that something terrible was wrong with her leg as she tried to move it. In the natural (what people can see with their physical eyes), it appeared as if she had torn some ligaments. Her leg immediately started swelling, but this is where living by faith can overcome something that seems impossible in the natural. This is why the Bible says in II Corinthians 5:7, *"For we walk by faith, not by sight."* The very first words out of her mouth were, "I am healed by the stripes of Jesus!" As she got up with obvious pain in her leg, the coach told a sub-runner to come take her place. She refused to accept the injury and said politely, but emphatically to the coach, "Healed people don't sit on the bench!" She not only stayed in the game, but by the time she rounded third base on the next hit, she had received her miracle. Nothing was broken or torn, and the pain was completely gone! Her words and her actions were in agreement with the faith of God that was in her heart, and a miracle was produced.

Think about all the things my wife could have spoken or done in that situation. She refused to be moved by what she saw or felt. She believed God and trusted Him for her healing. The key to receiving from God comes by believing His Word in your heart and saying it with your mouth. How does a person get saved? He believes in his heart and confesses Jesus as his Lord with the words of his mouth. The same way a person receives salvation spiritually is the same way a person receives physical healing, prosperity, peace, etc. You must believe it in your heart, and speak what you desire with the words of your mouth. When all your words and actions line up with the faith of God that is in your heart, you will receive 100% of the time.

Conclusion

Unbelief is the only hindrance to receiving from God. Knowing this truth empowers you to have a much closer walk with your Heavenly Father so you can accomplish His will in your life. Even the devil will be unable to stop you from fulfilling your God-given purpose. Nothing is impossible to God, and nothing will be impossible to you if you believe.

I encourage you to trust God with all your heart, all your strength, all your soul, and all your mind. God has given His very best for you. He has given you His all. When you give everything in your life to God, and *"trust Him with all your heart"*, you will experience a life here on the earth that is far above anything you could ever imagine. Jesus calls this

"The abundant life."

Prayer for Salvation

The most important decision you could ever make is accepting Jesus as the Lord and Savior of your life. Everything with God is easy, and in Romans 10:9-10, there are two things you must do to be born again: 1.) Confess with your mouth the Lord Jesus, and 2.) Believe in your heart that God raised Jesus from the dead.

If you are uncertain about your place in the kingdom of God, I want to help you find the assurance today of knowing that you belong eternally to Him. Say this simple prayer of salvation out loud:

"Lord Jesus, I believe you died for my sins on the cross and rose again. Right now, I confess with my mouth and

believe in my heart that you are the Lord of my life. From this day forward, I am a new person, and I thank you that I am now born again. Thank you for saving me and making my life new. Amen!"

Prayer for the Baptism of the Holy Spirit

The Baptism of the Holy Spirit, known also as "The Baptism of Fire", is separate from salvation and is available for every born-again Christian (Acts 2:39, Acts 8:14-17, Acts 19:1-6). It is essential for believers to receive the Baptism of the Holy Spirit so they can operate in the same power and anointing in which Jesus operated. According to Luke 11:13, there is only one thing a Christian must do to receive the Holy Spirit in his life: Ask. If you have never received the Baptism of the Holy Spirit, pray this simple prayer out loud:

"Holy Spirit, I ask you right now to come and dwell on the inside of me. I thank you for filling me with your anointing and your power, and I submit myself to your comfort and your guidance in the Name of Jesus. Amen!"

LaVergne, TN USA
15 March 2011
220205LV00001BB/2/P